Help! I'm a Gifted and Talented Teenager!

Mentoring insights for staff, parents and teens

Caroline Hiorns

Published in 2016 by Caroline Hiorns
Edited by Charlotte Hiorns

A catalogue record for this book is available from the British Library

ISBN 978-0-9934941-0-9

Typeset by Geoff Fisher
geoff.fisher@yahoo.co.uk

Printed and Bound in Great Britain by
CPI Books (UK) Croydon CR0 4YY

To Noel whose journey is my inspiration

About the Author

Caroline's interest in Gifted and Talented started with the struggles of her eldest son. A fascination with learning and countless conversations with gifted pupils as a governor and learning mentor have led to her mentoring questionnaire. She has wide mentoring experience across eight schools and colleges, most recently with gifted disadvantaged pupils. She has written on 'Emotional resilience – the key to success' for Optimus Education and run workshops for Potential Plus UK on 'Parenting a G and T child'. Caroline also runs workshops for staff, pupils and parents, full details of which are available at www.gifted-teens.wix.com/mentoring.

Caroline Miorns

July 2021

Contents

Foreword by Denise Yates, Chief Executive Potential Plus UK (formerly The National Association for Gifted Children)

How often do we ask the children or young people we support just how they work best, their hopes and dreams for the future and what is stopping them from maximising their potential? Not often enough I suspect; perhaps a hurried meeting just before a parents' evening or a group careers session where all the children look to see what others are going to say.

Yet giving every child or young person an ongoing opportunity to work with someone else on a one-to-one basis over a period of weeks can have a measurable impact on their achievement levels in schools. For example, The Education Endowment Toolkit produced by The Education Endowment Foundation and The Sutton Trust estimates that a period of mentoring can help to increase the average academic progress made by a student by at least one month and probably double that for a student from a disadvantaged background.

So mentoring helps. I know from our work with gifted and talented children (those with high learning potential is the term we prefer) that adult-to-child or peer-to-peer mentoring can be an essential lifeline in unlocking the gifts and talents these young people possess and in tackling issues such as under-achievement in school.

One of the biggest myths with high potential learners is that just because they are highly able they will attain the best grades in their exams without support. It is essential to give them opportunities to explore their passion; inspiration and challenge in the classroom; the power to motivate themselves; the ability to work hard and the social and emotional strength to do it including the resilience to pick themselves up when they fail. All of these things need to be done within a supportive school environment which recognises that these high potential learners may indeed struggle with some subjects; that they may need help with such things as organising their time and confidence and that they also need a supportive home environment where parents and carers understand their child and can help keep them on track.

This is a tall order both for many schools with busy timetables and resources issues and also many parents and carers who would find it difficult to know where to start, particularly in the difficult teenage years.

Caroline's book therefore provides not only a framework for a one-to-one mentoring approach that could be implemented across the whole school but also a wonderful and refreshing insight into the mind of gifted and talented children; about what is stopping them from achieving success. Additionally it offers a very practical framework based on her personal experience about some of the solutions to the common problems faced by these high potential learners.

So who is this book for? Most definitely teaching and other school professionals from the SENCO to the G&T lead, Learning Support Assistants and any other school staff working to improve pupil attainment would benefit from reading it. Governors who could volunteer to be involved in a mentoring programme would also benefit from reading it. Parents and carers, I also believe, would additionally benefit, but in a different way, by using some of the practical solutions to the issues outlined in this book.

However, my initial reaction when I finished the last page was to jump up and give it to all those children with high learning potential out there who often feel so isolated and who do not believe in the gifts they have because of barriers they face to achieving what they are capable of. They may lack confidence, be frightened because they need time to ponder a question that they may not be as bright as they thought they were, be disorganised and unable to revise for exams, be highly sensitive or concerned with justice and fairness which can cloud their learning or even have no space to discuss or get excited about the 'big questions' they want to ask. For me, if even one of these children realise that they are not on their own and that there are practical solutions to the issues they face, this book will have been a success.

If you have a mentoring programme or a programme for your high ability students, I suggest you look seriously at the framework suggested in this book and implement it.

Denise Yates

Acknowledgements

Although this book took a relatively short time to write it has been growing inside me for ten years or more and many people have contributed to it through their encouragement, wise words and teaching.

To start at the beginning, I am indebted to Noel whose willingness to talk and listen helped me to understand the plight of the G and T teen and led to my first steps in meeting this need.

To Jane, the inspirational head teacher who taught me so much about learning and pupil voice during my time as a primary governor.

To Danny who started me off on mentoring and, together with John, allowed me to develop my questionnaire in secondary schools.

To Beverley who is wonderful at asking big questions and helping me to bounce ideas around.

To Julie at Potential Plus who shares my passion for supporting G and T youngsters and to Denise for writing such a wonderful foreword.

To Eileen for encouragement to write ('the book inside you just has to come out!') and to Eileen, Genny and Ben for giving up some of their valuable summer holiday to read my manuscript.

To the many young people I have mentored who have taught me so much about their needs, fears and concerns and have developed such ingenious answers to their issues. My special thanks are due to Laura, Charlotte, Hannah, Izabella and Jennifer who have been so encouraging about the benefits of mentoring.

To Geoff Fisher who patiently guided me through the typesetting process.

To the friends who have supported me along the way, listening to my ideas, sharing their experiences, offering suggestions and with whom I have drunk coffee on so many occasions: Sally, Vanessa, Jane, Louise, Hazel, Darlene, Jackie and to Frances for the brain-storming walks.

To my housegroup who have shown constant interest in my G and T journey and given me such encouragement and for their prayers.

To my Dad the source of my fascination with education and my number one fan, to my sister Penney for her many insights and to my Mum.

Last and most importantly to Peter, Charlotte, Noel, Lydia and Isaac, my family, walking with me through the very many ups and downs of my G and T journey and believing in the value of my work. I am particularly grateful for the lessons each of my children has taught me about their needs, for their encouragement when I have struggled to be heard ('Mum, G and T is what you do') to Charlotte for the many hours she has spent expertly editing my work, to Lydia and Isaac for the cover design and to Peter who has picked me up so very many times and who has always been there for me.

Introduction

Gifted young people have the world at their fingertips, they have immense potential. Why then can certain situations cause them to stumble, fall and worse, sometimes even give up altogether?

Our eldest son, a high achiever, was like a cat in headlights when tackling various situations - he froze. At other times he became disheartened, frustrated and desperately unhappy, for a period even experiencing clinical depression. Our eldest daughter, an extremely hard worker and high achiever, lost all motivation, following an unexpectedly low AS result. It was weeks before she regained her ability to study.

As a concerned parent I walked with my children through these periods, listening when required and offering advice when they were able to take it. Over time, I realised from conversations with other parents in my role as G and T governor, that these phenomena were common to many gifted youngsters. Fascinated, I offered to work as a voluntary learning mentor with a number of pupils, which allowed me to listen a lot, explore with them their learning needs and tackle together any barriers they faced. I was delighted to be able to do this in both primary and secondary settings.

As a result I developed a 1:1 mentoring/coaching model which has further helped me understand that gifted pupils have their own individual learning needs and often are not gifted learners. Indeed, they have three major needs:

1. Gifted young people need a voice, a listening ear. They can become confused, isolated and debilitated by perfectionism. We need to understand them for who they are.

2. These young people need to fully understand their learning needs and to have permission to be a partner in their own learning.

3. These young people require sufficient resilience to become effective problem-solvers both now and in the future. This has to be gained by the provision of opportunities, which allow them to struggle and maybe 'fail' safely, and by explicit teaching of relevant skills and strategies.

Over the years I have had the opportunity to talk to many parents and it is clear that they also need information and support to enable them to effectively fulfil their vital parental support role.

My on-going mentoring work has convinced me of the positive impact of mentoring on the emotional well-being of the gifted pupil. A surprisingly small amount of time and support can impact greatly on results and the fulfilment of potential. This, in turn with careful cascading, will impact positively on other learners.

The purpose of this book is to outline issues faced by these young people and to share case studies that illustrate real perspectives on a particular barrier to learning and suggest possible solutions. These will undoubtedly address some other learning issues in the process. Each pupil has his or her own distinct needs but I hope that the range of illustrations will enable you, the teacher, tutor, mentor, ementor, G and T co-ordinator, parent or teen to find inspiration to reflect on and resolve whatever barriers they, or you, face.

Who and How?

Throughout this book I have chosen to use the term 'gifted' to describe the pupils whom I have mentored. One or two were exceptionally gifted but the vast majority will be similar to the G and T cohort found in secondary schools across the country. It is the academically gifted who I have found have benefited most from mentoring, as it is this group that experiences many of the issues listed below.

- Perfectionism
- High expectation of others
- Ability taken for granted
- How to accept and deal with areas of weakness, 'failure' – Feel they should understand and be able to do everything quickly
- Sensitivity
- Inability to ask for help
- Low self-esteem
- Feelings of isolation and confusion
- Frustration
- Lack of motivation
- Struggle to deal with many ideas
- Astute over how to solve learning issues but feel powerless to do so
- Organisation problems
- Lack of challenge
- Unanswered questions
- Inability to see big picture i.e. relevance of learning due to bite-size learning
- Poor memory
- Teaching style of lesson too limiting
- Problems with group learning
- Fear of talking to teachers or other adults

Talented pupils are often also gifted and they too will benefit. It is important to realise that these pupils may ultimately wish to pursue their talents rather than their academic strengths and there are many wonderful opportunities for them to do so. It is crucial that they are not made to feel as though this is a 'lesser' choice. Talented pupils however, *per se*, may not be gifted and so may not experience the same learning issues as the academically gifted. Mentoring, with its personalised focus, successfully addresses emotional and learning issues faced by a range of gifted young people including the disadvantaged. A full list of groups with whom it can be successfully used is included at the end in the section 'Over to You'. Here you will also find a detailed account of how to set up a mentoring scheme to embed it in the school learning structure so that impact is maximised. Communication is the key. I have relied heavily on contact with a school link teacher whose role is outlined in this section and whose help is instanced in a number of case studies throughout this book.

The Questionnaire – My Invaluable Assessment Tool

When I first started mentoring I used some very general questions given to me by a local mentor, which focussed mainly on aspiration and careers. At the same time, the primary school where I was a governor was doing some research into children's learning using Guy Claxton's learning power mind, as outlined in his book *Building Learning Power*. I was fascinated by the impact of his ideas on the pupils including my own children, so decided to use his learning mind diagram as an initial talking point in my mentoring sessions. It was very helpful. I soon found, however, that it did not pinpoint all of the issues faced by gifted pupils.

So, I expanded the focus, at the same time turning it into a series of statements, as I was very aware that many gifted pupils thought they were unique in experiencing some of their issues or did not recognise them as such and a statement allowed them to reflect on where they really were. I also added the questions at the beginning and the end of the questionnaire and at the end of each section. These allowed me to quickly get to know the mentees. The introductory questions were a gentle way of starting the process. The question at the end of each section broke up the statement rating so the mentee did not go into automatic pilot when circling them. In fact I take back the questionnaire at the end of each section and pose the question myself so that the mentee has more space to reflect aloud. I then note down the outcome of our dialogue. The section 'Other factors' has proved very helpful in highlighting issues that may not otherwise have come to light, if at all, until several sessions later but that can often impact greatly on performance.

Over time I have refined the questionnaire to remedy wording that proved to be ambiguous and to include statements exploring any other issue that regularly presented itself. The most recent change has been the inclusion of the statement on exams. Through conversation with friends I have become increasingly aware that certain gifted youngsters suffer from a virtual phobia of exams, which cumulatively impacts ever more negatively on performance. I have decided to include reference to exams to explore how widespread this is and to encourage mentees to seek help if necessary.

As I have worked through the questionnaire with my mentees and unpicked their initial scoring we have highlighted all sorts of areas in which they need advice or a strategy to go forwards. We have worked together to find these. Sometimes this has proved difficult and I have often thought it would be helpful to have a book of stories and possible solutions to which I could refer when necessary. Fortunately, as time has gone on, I have been able to use wisdom gained in past sessions with new mentees. Each mentee is different, as are their particular circumstances, but often the nub of one solution is highly useful in developing the kernel of another. I hope that you will find the plethora of stories described in the case studies will provide an invaluable stimulus in your own problem-solving whether you are a new mentor, a very busy teacher or wishing to expand your personal understanding and store of ideas. Case studies describe my real experiences as a mentor or are based on truth. Most names and some specific details have been changed to assure anonymity. Each story, though individual, is often voiced by other mentees although the exact details may differ.

Mentoring Questionnaire

About you

1. What are your strengths in school or out?

2. What are your weaknesses in school or out?

3. What are your interests?

4. What are your aspirations?

5. Which subjects are you studying?

6. Which do you enjoy most?

Key (circle the number)
0 = totally lacking
1 = not very good
2 = fairly good
3 = pretty good
4 = good
5 = excellent

About your learning

Resilience

I feel good about myself	0	1	2	3	4	5
I am happy about the expectation others have of me	0	1	2	3	4	5
I am good at keeping going when I am stuck	0	1	2	3	4	5
I often take risks in my learning	0	1	2	3	4	5
I see mistakes as learning opportunities	0	1	2	3	4	5
I never feel stressed or pressurised	0	1	2	3	4	5
I am a perfectionist	0	1	2	3	4	5
I am sensitive	0	1	2	3	4	5
I am confident	0	1	2	3	4	5
Teachers often praise my learning	0	1	2	3	4	5
I cope well with exams	0	1	2	3	4	5
I am good at managing distractions	0	1	2	3	4	5
I learn best when it is quiet	0	1	2	3	4	5
Learning at school is interesting	0	1	2	3	4	5

What would you like to learn about?

Resourcefulness

I am good at time management	0	1	2	3	4	5
I always meet deadlines	0	1	2	3	4	5
I manage long-term projects well	0	1	2	3	4	5
I manage my homework well	0	1	2	3	4	5
I ask big questions	0	1	2	3	4	5
I sometimes do not understand my learning	0	1	2	3	4	5
Learning is often challenging	0	1	2	3	4	5
Learning is well paced	0	1	2	3	4	5
I get frustrated by the learning at school	0	1	2	3	4	5
I am inspired by the learning at school	0	1	2	3	4	5
I often find I already know what I am taught	0	1	2	3	4	5

What could you teach us?

Reflectiveness

I am good at ideas	0	1	2	3	4	5
Learning is sufficiently deep and broad	0	1	2	3	4	5
I have a good memory	0	1	2	3	4	5
The style of teaching and learning suits me	0	1	2	3	4	5
I see how learning in class fits together	0	1	2	3	4	5
I know how individual subjects fit the big picture	0	1	2	3	4	5

How could we make school/learning even better?

Reciprocity

Pupils are kind at school	0	1	2	3	4	5
I have a good group of friends	0	1	2	3	4	5
I enjoy learning in a group	0	1	2	3	4	5
I talk about my learning with my teachers	0	1	2	3	4	5

What have you learnt from other pupils?

Other factors

Do you have enough sleep?

Do you have a balanced diet?

Do you drink enough water?

Do you do regular exercise?

Do you have a quiet place to work?

Do you talk through your learning at home?

Do you have particular learning needs?

Do you have particular medical needs?

Do you have family/friend issues?

What would you like to gain from the mentoring sessions?

Inspired by Guy Claxton's Learning Power mind and developed by Caroline Hiorns for the particular needs of G and T following numerous conversations over many years with G and T teenagers and their parents.

About You

What are your strengths in school or out?

For many young people this is a very good place to start. They are quick to tell me their strengths in the school setting; maths, English, drama. Out of school skills are also often easy to recall, particularly sporting or musical ones. However, when it comes to personal attributes or learning skills they often need a bit of encouragement.

However, for some young people, notably those with low self-esteem, the under-achiever or perhaps the quiet ones, this proves more difficult and sometimes impossible. Posing the question another way can help; what would your friends or your family say? 'I am a good friend' may be as far as they are prepared initially to commit themselves. As this section is meant to put them at their ease, it may then be best to suggest they go and ask their friends and family what they think and report back next time. Any strengths they have mentioned are a useful springboard for future positive progress.

Case study 1

As soon as Sophie (year 13) entered the room she began to pour out her difficulties about writing a personal statement for her UCAS form and voice her doubts about whether she would actually achieve a place anyway. Having reassured her that we would work on this next time if she brought it along with her, I suggested that we go through the questionnaire as this would help me to get to know her and enable me to help her better. Her response to what are your strengths in school and out was met with a list of things she was not good at. Having written these down as answers to the next question, I asked her again to name a strength. She thought for a very long while and finally came up with 'I am a good loyal friend'. I suggested that as a target she ask her family and friends and also before she went to sleep at night she reflect on a good thing that happened that day or a personal strength.

The next time she came to mentoring she had not yet managed to come up with any further strengths but she brought along her 'final' attempt at her personal statement. As time was now short we spent the session editing it. What was most apparent was her inability to sing her praises. We spent a long time considering each sentence and removing any apologetic phrases. The finished version made her smile. 'It's still me' she said 'but a positive me.' It was not the best personal statement I had ever read but it clearly reflected the positive traits of her personality and simply stated her desire to study languages. To her surprise the offers started to roll in.

The following session she arrived with her boyfriend who I was also mentoring and asked if he could come in. I decided to allow this as a one off, on the understanding that this was her session and I expected her to still engage in discussion with me. We talked through how her work was going and in particular her A level revision for her January exams and she told me it was going well and described how she had approached it. Then we came to her strengths. I decided that as Jack was present I would ask him to comment. He told me that when she started something she carried it through, she was easy to get on with and put lots of effort into her work. Sophie began to squirm but I praised her and asked for some examples. She told me about her work in a café where she worked hard and did well by talking to the customers at length. So, we began to add to her list of strengths.

What are your weaknesses in school or out?

Interestingly mentees rarely mention particular school subjects in this category so when they do I always explore the reasons. Much more commonly they list lack of confidence, poor organisation, low motivation and distractions, all of which are covered later in the questionnaire. Quite a few also mention not speaking out in class unless asked, talking to new people or to an audience, performing.

Two particular misconceptions I have discovered by asking this question are that if you have to work hard then you cannot really be gifted. One year 10 told me that she was not naturally intelligent so she revised a lot to combat this. The other misconception is that if you cannot do something quickly then you are not good at it and that your ability is determined by the comparative speed of the whole class. Both misconceptions sadly foster low-esteem and create stress in struggling to overcome it. Sometimes they also cause young people to abandon subjects at which, with concerted effort, they could be very good and benefit greatly from the process of perseverance.

Case study 2

Anna (year 10) identified a weakness in Spanish. She wanted to improve her confidence and achievement as her grades were much lower than in other subjects. I asked her if she knew why. She did. Her teacher always spoke in Spanish and she just did not understand, which scared her. Was her teacher aware I wondered? Having ascertained that she found him approachable, I suggested her target was to speak to him at an appropriate moment and ask if he could suggest a way forward.

At our next session, two weeks later, I learnt that, determined not to lose her nerve, she had done this straightaway. The teacher had gladly recommended two helpful web-sites. Anna had bought a pad and a file and set about doing some of the exercises on the sites that the teacher had kindly marked. He was therefore aware on which grammar constructions she was working and so could direct relevant questions to her in class. She was able to answer, sometimes with help. Her confidence soared. Anna's mum was delighted as now she could help her daughter by encouraging her to use these sites whereas before she had felt powerless. The class also benefited as the teacher then recommended these resources to them. When Anna took her next speaking assessment her grade went from a D to a B. She was no longer scared of Spanish.

Buoyed up by this success, Anna set about conquering anxieties in other subjects by independently exploring possible solutions.

Case study 3

Tom (year 10) told me he was not good at public speaking. We explored this statement together. He was happy to ask questions in class unless he thought it was a stupid question, in which case he asked his neighbour. He was also happy to read out a piece of good work unless he was asked to stand up. This unnerved him as he felt on show. He assured me that other pupils did not laugh at him and he was happy with his preparation and the quality of his work. He was also fine in group presentations but on his own his face went really red, he got hot and tended to speed up. I suggested that in his presentation in sports studies the next day he take along a drink to sip, take a deep breath and take his time as he spoke. He also said he would talk to his English teacher for tips as she was good at presentations.

At our next session he reported that his face again went red when he started his presentation but he paused, took a breath and the red subsided. He only felt a little bit hot. I congratulated him and reassured him that this would get better over time. He told me that he had also spoken to his big brother who used to go red and so takes deep breaths and focusses. However, he had not spoken to his teacher. (In fact his English teacher was my school contact and I had a termly review with her the next day so I told her to expect his question. She said that she herself got very nervous when speaking and so was delighted that he saw her as skilled at presentations. Tom never did speak to her but after our conversation she was able to quietly help build his confidence).

Our next target was for Tom to come and give me a presentation without Powerpoint. As he had forgotten I gave him a few minutes to think through his weekend, a topic with which he would be very familiar. The first time he spoke he remained seated, made no eye contact and fiddled with his hair. The second time around he stood and spoke much more confidently, making eye contact but this time he had his hands in his pockets. His next target was to practice in front of a mirror.

Before the next session I thought hard about how to give Tom further expert advice on presenting. I had recently been to an event that used a clip from Ted Talks (www.ted.com/talks). So I researched a few that dealt with topics I thought would interest him. We watched excerpts from these together and I got him to analyse why they were successful. It was striking how much space each speaker allowed himself and also the use made of humour to draw in the listener. I encouraged him to look at some more at home. As we had been focussing on public speaking for quite some time we then decided it was time to look at another area for improvement.

At the beginning of the next school year I was asked to recommend a couple of my mentees to speak to prospective mentees about the value of the scheme. I recommended Tom. Yes, he went slightly red but he spoke with confidence and ease and afterwards was smiling broadly at his achievement.

Case study 4

James (year 4) was quick to tell me how good he was at maths. He also did not hesitate in highlighting English, particularly writing, as an area of weakness. I wondered how he knew.

'Well', he said, 'it takes me a long time to do a page of writing but I can do a page of hard sums really quickly'.

'So', I said, 'if you do something slowly does that mean you are not good at it?'

'Yes!' he responded, incredulously.

As a target I asked him to go away and do a mini-research project on an inventor and then to come and tell me what they invented and how long they took. He chose Alexander Graham Bell.

At the next session he came and spoke to me about Bell and explained that it took him quite some years and lots of different attempts to achieve the transmission of sound. This time it was my turn to be incredulous. Why, I wondered did it take him so long, was he being stupid? James was clear that this was not the case and that Bell was indeed an extremely clever man.

'So', I asked James, 'if Bell took a long time to achieve his goal and he is regarded as ingenious, why do you think you should be able to do everything quickly, and you are not good at anything you cannot?'. The penny dropped.

I have used this story many times with subsequent mentees who equate ability with speed and think this is unchangeable. We then set about addressing the barriers to success step by step.

What are your interests?

This question is important in that it allows the mentees to talk in a relaxed way about their life out of school and allows me to glimpse the 'real' them.

Favourite interests are sports, often involving membership of school or county teams, making or listening to music, watching a variety of television programmes, reading, playing computer games and often baking. I have learnt a lot about a range of television programmes, types of music and literature, and they enjoy helping me to enter their world.

It is also very illuminating to discover which mentees only do solitary activities, those who are involved in voluntary work or positions of leadership and those who have a real passion for something.

Some mentees do very little out of school except school work, thinking this is the best way to ensure a successful future. They are often very intense. I find it helpful to explain that future success will be increased if they develop the whole person. Universities are keen on rounded personalities who know how to play as well as to work and who have mechanisms that allow them to relax. I have found it helpful to use the two following diagrams to inspire those who do not seem to have any interests or hobbies. It is important to ensure that at least some of the ideas suggested do not involve a cost.

Mentees can then make their own 'My interests, activities and hobbies' diagram as described at the end of the book under 'Three useful diagrams'.

Case study 5

Chloe (year 10) told me her interests were spending time with friends at weekends, reading and making cakes or desserts when work allowed, which was usually at half-term. She also gave herself the highest score for stress. I suggested that she take up an activity to aid relaxation. She responded that she intended to support a good cause when she was in the sixth form and then do some voluntary work in a hospital as she wanted to be a medic.

I created the two diagrams for her and at the next session asked her to choose something from both. She decided she would like to read, do art or garden and, as a group activity, play board games like Articulate, Boggle or Scrabble. Her target was to engage in one from each section over the up-coming holiday. After Easter she reported that she was reading *Lord of The Rings* but was not finding lots of time. I suggested a little every night just before sleep. She had also played games on Easter Sunday as a family, which she had greatly enjoyed. Exams then took over and she did not find time to read but she did watch a little television.

After the exams we started to look at the requirements for being a medic. We noted that, under the non-academic requirements, St Andrew's University listed positions of responsibility, organisational ability, interests and hobbies, cultural and sporting activities and achievements and social involvement. I had also spoken to the admissions officer from Lancaster University who had informed me that excellence in non-academic areas shows you can relax and yet still get good academic grades, you can manage many demands.

Chloe created 'Three useful diagrams' (see pp. 127–31) and also started to put together one showing how she fulfilled the requirements of a good medic. She decided it was time to start to broaden her interests and so determined over the holiday to research different art styles, which would also be helpful for her art GCSE. She also intended to take up sewing by talking to her Nan.

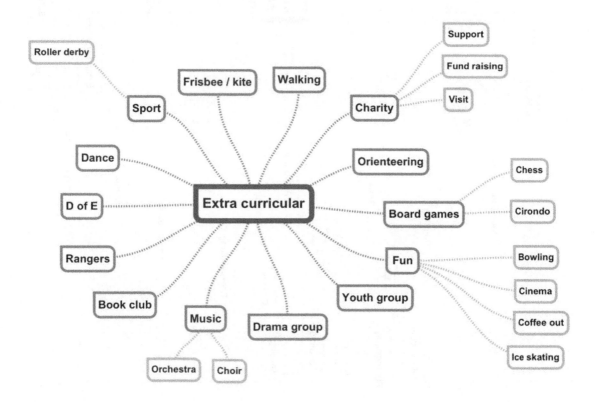

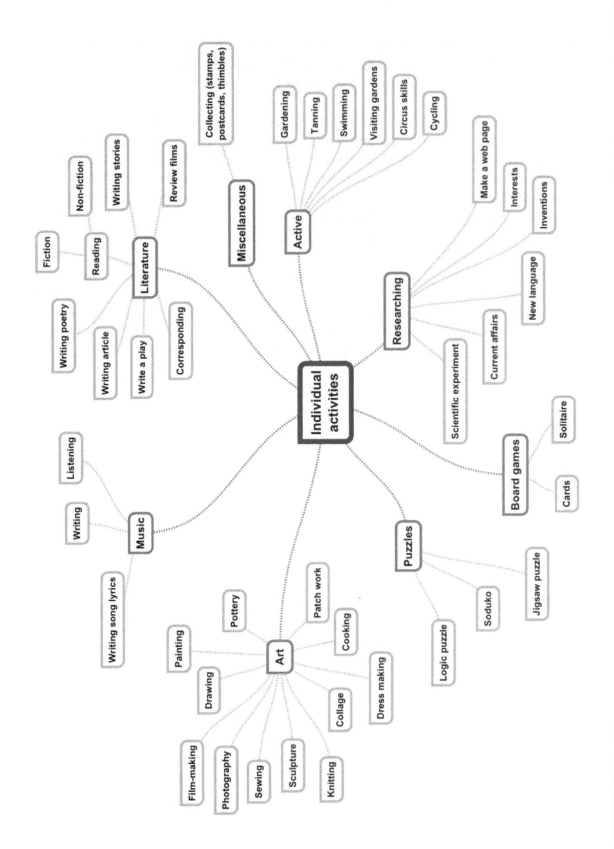

What are your aspirations?

Many of my mentees, particularly in key stage 4, have no idea yet what they would like to do or be in the future. I reassure them that this is quite normal and very helpful as it means their minds are still open to the many varied possibilities on offer. For some of them starting to open up future courses is a wonderful source of motivation to hard work as they realise what it takes to be able to access these. Some however do have a strong idea of where their future lies but usually I find it is not more than that, an idea. In either case their answer to this question can be a useful springboard to future progress.

Case study 6

Emily (year 10) had already told me in response to the earlier question about interests that she loved to write stories and articles and indeed, in year 6, had made a monthly magazine for her class encouraging everyone to contribute. Her aspiration was to be a writer. She was particularly inspired by Jacqueline Wilson's life story. She explained that she started lots of stories but rarely finished them. Her mother had suggested she show her best writing to her teacher. We decided this would be her next target. In fact at that moment she was co-writing a book with her friend, so we agreed she would show it to her teacher. We also started to look at Literary Festivals around the country to see what events they ran and when they took place.

By the next session Emily had given her book to the teacher to read and we set the target that she would ask my school contact, also an English teacher, if she could start a school magazine.

Over the next few sessions she kept me up to date as her teacher finished her book and fixed a time to give Emily and her co-writer some useful feedback. My link teacher also spoke to her to suggest she set up a blog as this could be added to on an on-going basis and would not be limited by publication dates.

After the exams I was able to recommend a short story competition run by IGGY (International Global and Gifted Youth) to Emily. She was really delighted by the flexibility of the title and challenged by the parameters of time and length and proudly sent me her finished entry for perusal.

I continued to mentor Emily over a longer period as part of a mixed programme of provision in which I was involved at that time. She did not win the competition but greatly enjoyed the thrill of entering and subsequently found another competition to enter. This, she found, helped her to raise her aspirations. I was able to recommend a young writers' club I discovered at the local library, which allowed her to link up with other writers of a similar age and, at the same time, she decided to increase her knowledge of classical literature. Her aspiration was now much more than just a dream, she was well on her way to achieving it.

Case study 7

Jess (year 10) told me her aspiration was to be successful, maybe in property or interior design. She was a delightful pupil but it quickly became clear that she was not a risk taker, preferring to stay within known areas and to do what she knew she could do. I decided it would be good to introduce her to the breadth of study options.

At the next session I brought along a selection of university prospectuses chosen from the top 40 according to the Guardian league table. She selected one. I asked her to work through all the courses offered and to call out any which interested her or of which she had never heard. I noted them down. I then read the list back to her and she chose one to investigate in further depth.

Her task was to explore several things; what the course was about, what A levels were essential to access it, what grades were needed and to what possible careers it could lead. Initially she struggled with how to extract all this information, particularly essential subjects. However, she soon realised that for many courses there are no prescribed A levels. Once we had explored one subject we then worked our way through others on her list. She was quite amazed at how many options there were and what variety existed. Following this task I set her a target to explore a different university online in her own time.

As a result of this task, Jess told me that she had realised she needed to up her game. She also needed to broaden her horizons. So she had now spoken to the English teacher about how to move from a B to an A in her writing. She had also decided that, as she liked music, she would start to explore a wider range of styles using a list of suggestions given to her by a friend. Her intention was to go to a diverse range of concerts. I was delighted that in her own way she was moving out of her comfort zone.

Which subjects are you studying? Which do you enjoy most?

These questions are really useful in getting to know the pupil. The information obtained at this stage allows mentoring targets to be set across the whole subject range. Otherwise some pupils keep very quiet in discussion about certain less favourite subject areas. It is also really interesting to see whether their favourite subjects influence their extra-curricular activities.

Occasionally the answers highlight potential issues. One year 10 boy told me that he loved maths but not when it was challenging. I had been told by my link teacher that he always came top in school in the maths challenge. Questions started to formulate in my head. (See his story under perfectionism). Often pupils tell me they like a subject as that is what they are good at. This is often a stepping stone to helping them use their confidence in their favourite subject to tackle a lack of it in another subject area.

On one occasion a pupil told me with great conviction that she did not like any of her subjects. I was quite surprised as she was very articulate and reflective. However, when we later came to the question on what would you like to study she enthusiastically replied 'Oh loads of things! Psychology, Politics ...' Subsequent discussion revealed a total lack of motivation for school which was showing itself in repeated lateness. I was able to draw this dichotomy to the attention of the school so that they could investigate further. For my part I brought along some university prospectuses to allow the pupil to explore other possible areas of interest. This allowed us to draw up a list of her choosing and to then explore issues and articles from several courses to start to build enthusiasm. I emailed the list of subjects in which she was interested to my link teacher so that the school could also use it to support her.

Case study 8

Josh (year 4) was a highly reflective boy. He was determined to do as well as he could and pondered how to achieve this. One session he came to me and said that he always took a long time doing his maths homework but he had noticed that his friend Daniel seemed to be able to work much more quickly. He had also been thinking about art and wondered how he could become interested in it. He set himself the target of talking to different friends to find their tips and ideas. The next session he came in with a big beam on his face. He had talked to Daniel and was now getting his homework done much more quickly and had been given some ideas by another friend who was good at art, which he hoped would increase his enjoyment.

I was very impressed with his proactivity and have shared his technique with other mentees.

Case study 9

Lauren (year 10) knew high grades were important and worked very hard but only put in minimal effort at anything that was not directly related to future results. She particularly enjoyed French but certainly did not enjoy science. In a bid to boost her enjoyment I suggested she talk to others in her class who liked science. She assured me that there were very few people who did but agreed to ask anyway. At the next session she told me she had asked a lad who said he liked the way it linked to other stuff. She accepted this fact but repeated that she did not find it stimulating. 'Although' she added, 'I do enjoy watching certain science programmes on TV, particularly about space.' I left it at that and decided to try and build on her enjoyment of French.

In our final session, as we reviewed progress, Lauren suddenly said 'I like science now.' She explained that she found chemistry really interesting and was enjoying the astronomy part of physics though not friction. She now understood it more. I have since learnt that she has decided to do sciences for A level with a view to a possible medical career.

About your learning

Resilience

Resilience is generally the area mentees find the hardest. Gifted pupils are often so used to grasping concepts easily, to getting things right, to achieving highly that when learning gets harder, particularly as they progress up the school, they begin to flounder. They do not cope well with 'failure', as they see it, they have not developed the necessary strategies. However, it is certain that ultimately they will fail at something in life: a test, an exam, an Oxbridge application, a job interview. It is imperative they learn how to cope with this and how to bounce back as early as possible so that they do not give up altogether in the face of adversity.

'Many professionals are almost always successful at what they do and rarely experience failure. And because they have rarely failed, they have never learned how to learn from failure. Whenever their learning strategies go wrong, they become defensive, screen out criticism and "put the blame" on anyone and everyone but themselves. In short, their ability to learn shuts down at precisely the moment they need it most.' (*Teaching smart people how to learn* C. Argyris, 2008.)

I feel good about myself

Most of my mentees grade themselves at 3 or above for this statement but a small minority score 2 or even 1. What are the reasons for this? Transition is a major factor, particularly at the beginning of year 12 or 13 where pupils often feel guilty as they do not immediately seem able to achieve at the levels they did at GCSE. If this is not voiced and addressed in year 12 and consequently AS grades are not as expected, pupils become desperate and often see themselves as incapable of high A level success. It can become a self-fulfilling prophesy or they lower their expectations so as not to be disappointed. As one mentee told me, 'failing to meet my targets is the worst feeling in the world'. Poor results can also lead some to become the victim and blame the school, the exam board and to make excuses for their short-comings rather than seeking a way forward. Then there are those who get an unexpectedly low AS result even though they have worked really hard and been assured by the school they would do really well.

Low self-esteem is also the product of family issues, such as parental separation or where pupils feel they are unable to talk through their concerns and feelings with a parent or a teacher and so may assume they are the only one who does not understand their learning. This may also be a passing phase as they are going through an anxious time when they complete the questionnaire, perhaps changing subject options or following a particularly challenging test.

Case study 10

Megan (year 13) graded her self-esteem at 1. She explained that she used to be an A/A* student but shortly before she took her GCSEs she achieved mostly Bs and became demoralised. Now she was a B/C student. Her boyfriend encouraged her but she found it difficult to talk things through at home. Her mum was very happy to do so but Megan felt she was very different in character to her. She was much more like her Dad but he seemed to deal with things on his own. I suggested that she talk to him to find out how he tackled anxiety and stress.

Megan had major anxieties about her coursework. Her next history essay was due in that week and her English essays were not going well. We started to unpick her concerns. I assured her that we could find a solution. She needed to believe progress was possible and to take control of the situation.

It transpired that she had already made the notes for her history essay and could usually write what she saw as an A/B essay but this time it just was not working. She didn't understand why and time was running out. She knew her teachers had confidence in her but maybe she was afraid of letting them down. Unusually she had been awake until two in the morning. I explained that occasionally creativity just does not flow and enquired if she had thought of asking for a short extension. This was not something she had considered but she agreed to do so.

Megan was struggling with her English essays. She had two teachers and one marked in red and wrote a lot of comments and suggestions on each essay. Megan found it really difficult to take them all on board. I suggested she talk to this teacher, quietly tell her how she was feeling and ask if she could use another colour to mark and make just a few comments each time. Megan had half-planned a number of essays for the other teacher but had stopped as she did not fully understand the question. When this had happened before, she had asked for help and been given some useful tips but did not feel she could ask again. I assured her this was possible and that teachers welcomed pupils who were keen to perfect their work.

Megan came to the next session much happier. She had spoken to her Dad who said that when he had loads of issues he made a prioritised list and then worked through ticking them off. Megan had started to try this to good effect. The first English teacher was now using green and making a small number of helpful comments. The other teacher had helped her to pick apart an essay title and had worked an example with her. This was not the end of the story. We spent several more sessions thinking about how Megan could be a proactive partner in her learning, she gradually realised that ability and success are not fixed, she could influence the outcome. A very valuable lesson!

Case study 11

Our daughter Charlotte is a highly conscientious, hard-working and driven student. Her aim is to achieve as highly as possible. At parents' evening staff complimented her on her work ethic and told us she was assured of some wonderful results. It came as a complete shock therefore when I opened the envelope containing her AS results, as she was on holiday with a friend, and had to tell her that her spoken French had been scored as a low C and so she had achieved a B overall. She was devastated. Distance made me powerless to help. In her eyes she had failed.

When term began again, as the school were mystified by this result, I suggested she ask for a remark. It came back with the same grade, even though on the tape of her spoken exam her speech was highly confidant and fluent. We now had a daughter who felt incapable. It was as though she was going through a 'mini-depression,' as she put it she had 'shut down'. Charlotte had given of her best and the goal posts seemed to have changed. It took weeks for her to be able to regain motivation. The school were very supportive, giving her space and building her confidence. She decided to retake in January, which was then a possibility. On the exam day, our normally healthy Charlotte, who had hardly missed a day of school, was in bed in the midst of a virulent flu bug that was sweeping the school. She went in just for her exam but came back telling me that she had been unable to think straight. In March she achieved an A.

Charlotte's experience is not unique. I have encountered a number of students who have received unexpectedly low results, some through exam board inconsistencies, some through errors on the day, some due to school or college errors. These results can really floor a student. In Charlotte's case it was the first time she had experienced 'failure'. It is vital to provide students with support and a listening ear, to encourage them to be kind to themselves and to allow time to recover.

Case study 12

Hannah (year 10) gave herself a 2 for self-esteem. When I enquired why, she told me that she thought everyone else in her class was better than her and she should not be there. This was especially true in science and art. I wondered what gave her this impression. She told me that in art she felt everyone else produced better work and in science she did not seem to get things when other pupils did. We decided to focus on art.

Hannah talked me through her current art project. She had already used quite a range of different media. I suggested she talk to her teacher to find the next step forward. By the next session Hannah had spoken to her teacher who had written some useful comments in the front of her art book and reassured her there was nothing to worry about. She had also encouraged her to use an even wider range of media. At the following session Hannah proudly showed me her artwork to date. She had started to use other media and discovered she was particularly good at watercolour, acrylic, pastels and drawing. Her interest grew. Hannah was greatly enjoying her chats with her teacher and she had been told that she was going from strength to strength. She now turned her attention to tackling her lack of confidence in science.

This time I asked her what she would suggest. Hannah decided to learn the key words and equations and to start reading through the revision book. This had an immediate impact on her self-belief in science and her next assessment grade was significantly higher.

I am happy about the expectations others have of me

'A bright boy like you should be able to do this!' This was the remark made to our son Noel when he was about 12 by a concerned teacher who was trying to help him believe in his ability. Sadly it caused great anxiety. He found coming up with ideas in creative writing really hard. The blank white page unnerved him. It took a lot of encouragement to finally ask this teacher for help. Gifted young people, just like other pupils, have things they find hard, things they feel unable to do. One year 10 mentee told me that when he was lower down the school, French was his favourite lesson and he got top marks. Now he was more interested in business and spent a lot of time on homework and at an extra-curricular club in this field. He felt demoralised when, after coming third in the class (something which I think he had worked out for himself), the French teacher said she expected more of him. He had already achieved a highly respectable grade.

Most of my mentees are happy with the expectations of others but for some these are too high or too low, which can cause frustration or stress. Several pupils find it hard to believe they can do as well as their predicted targets but after talking through the idea of a step-by-step approach to progress they are usually reassured and much more positive. Some also find expectation raises the bar in a slightly scary way but rise to the challenge and are prepared to put in the effort. One year 13 told me that she believed she could meet her targets with a lot of hard work but, as she had achieved highly at GCSE, was concerned about letting her family down if her grades were not as expected. I have also found that those year 13s who do not cope well with transition to sixth form nor share their anxieties with anyone, often perform poorly at AS. They then feel high expectations are totally unrealistic and unachievable. A detailed analysis of their weaknesses and a step-by-step plan for progress is the way forward.

For some though, parental expectation is a major headache. I have several mentees who have told me that their Dad (it always seems to be a Dad!) did not do as well at school as he had hoped or did not have the opportunity to go to university so is determined that their son will do so. Consequently, when they achieve 98%, instead of congratulating them, Dad wants to know what happened to the other 2%. Likewise if they do not achieve the top grade for achievement on their report, he wants to know why, even when this is not possible as they have not yet covered all the necessary syllabus content. Generally I have no contact with the parents so these dilemmas are difficult to address. Something I have tried successfully is to hold a series of parent support groups for specific key stages or year groups. I give a short talk about common issues the pupil may be facing and provide a parent's perspective on ideas to address these, using real life stories from my own children or those I have met. This is then followed by a chance for parents to talk in groups or to circulate over refreshments. This is always very well received but the parents with the highest expectations do not always attend.

Occasionally mentees tell me that teacher expectation is too low resulting in frustration at the ceiling to learning. I work with them to find a way forward.

There is sometimes also a dichotomy between the expectations of school and those of family. One year 13 told me that her parents were from a working class background and did not go to university so they praised her, whatever mark she achieved. However her teachers expected a lot more, which caused her to panic. She added, 'I really wish my parents understood what I could achieve and how I felt about my grades so that they could support me when I am stressed or unhappy about not quite getting the marks I want'.

Case study 13

Matthew (year 10) agreed that teacher expectations were realistic except in science where teachers thought he could achieve more than he was. His Dad however had very high expectations wanting 100% in everything. He could not accept that his son could find anything difficult. I suggested that maybe we find a solution to please both teachers and Dad.

Matthew was very keen on reading, creative writing and music but science just did not interest him. He let slip when talking about challenge that he perhaps found science hard. Other pupils in his class spent about ten hours on their coursework but he spent one. In his class tests he did not do well, perhaps he should do more in-depth revision rather than simply skimming the revision book. This was a good moment to explain the need for good GCSE grades if he wanted to keep his future options open. He had not realised that the impression given by GCSE grades was important. We talked through the three sciences and I noted there were indeed some areas that interested him. He was currently studying a biology topic on muscles and muscle fatigue. So I asked him to find out three more facts and pose himself a wondering question. Next session he told me that he had looked on Google facts and found that you can run an electrical current through a muscle to move it as it imitates the brain signal and that muscles get energy from respiration. He had not posed himself a wondering question. Now he was studying cloning. I asked him to find out more facts about this using a different type of resource and to pose a wondering question. This time though he had to talk to his Dad about it to impress him with his knowledge. I explained that I had used this technique with another student and that she had become really interested in the area she had explored. Sadly, Matthew did not follow through with the target. I already knew he was very laid back. It was time to speak to my link teacher for her support. She was able to talk through with him the effort required of a mentee and to explain that others would be glad of the opportunity if he no longer wished to continue. Matthew became more enthusiastic to progress.

Case study 14

Samuel, a year 13 applying to university, had been predicted B for chemistry even though he had just managed to achieved A at AS. Despite several attempts he had been unable to get his teacher to alter the prediction. I suggested we turn this into a positive. Since he was so certain of his ability we would spend the year proving he was right. What was his strategy? To guarantee success he knew that he needed to revise better and to start earlier. He decided to do revision notes as he went along.

The coursework element was a scientific investigation of his own choosing in which he had to devise the experiment and order all the chemicals. He had to take full responsibility. This he found really hard as he liked constant reassurance. I reassured him this would be a wonderful opportunity to increase his resilience and resourcefulness.

Samuel worked well on his revision notes but the practical was a cause of great anxiety. The final practical investigation did not work but he still had to use the results he had obtained. Imagine his amazement when he achieved 42/45, an A! His explanations had made sense even though his testing went awry. Just like real life, I commented.

Revision proved hard as he struggled with distractions but his determination paid off. I saw him as he came out of the exam room smiling broadly. The exam had gone really well. On the day of the results he was ecstatic. He had got his A in chemistry. He had proved his teacher wrong. He was about to start his degree in chemistry with a research year in industry.

I am good at keeping going when I am stuck

My mentees have generally told me that they are good at keeping going when they are stuck. Some see this as a challenge and others say they never get stuck. However a few struggle with his concept. What is the reason? Some say they feel guilty and frustrated as others seem to get it and they think they ought to know. Others are lacking in self-confidence and so do not like to speak up. What is most concerning is that quite a number of this group do not ask a friend or puzzle it out at home but quietly leave the problem and hope the teacher will not notice. I can personally relate to this. My French teacher was very strict and expected us to understand immediately. So, in class tests, which we marked ourselves and then declared our score by a show of hands, I never admitted to my actual result. Instead I put up my hand with the majority and then worried afterwards. It was not until I was moved to the B set and a family friend offered to work with me building from the basics that I eventually improved and actually went on to take French at degree level. I work with all these mentees to help them find the way forward, which usually involves speaking to a teacher (either their current one or one of their choosing), or a friend or devising a strategy of their own.

Case study 15
Sophie, year 13, had extremely low self-esteem due to family breakup. This had been exacerbated by an unexpectedly low result in French the previous summer following a particularly hard exam. She was convinced that she would fare similarly in her next maths exam. She had chosen to focus on keeping going when she was stuck and I asked her what strategy she currently used when tackling a problem. I was impressed to hear she worked methodically through the process. However, when she got stuck she immediately stopped and contacted her teacher by email or spoke to her in class. As a target, I suggested that next time this happened, she try for 10 more minutes, experiencing and coping with the feelings of anxiety, and then if necessary seek help. At our next session she told me that this technique had allowed her to independently get further in her problems.

The exam was extremely hard and she felt like giving up but she tried the technique I had taught her and kept on going. When her result came out she achieved an A. Ecstatic does not do justice to her reaction!

I often take risks in my learning

Risk-taking is a wonderful way to grow resilience. However, many mentees are risk adverse, preferring to stay within their comfort zone and do what they know they can do. They often equate risk with danger and so feel the wisest thing to do is to avoid it. We spend a few minutes laughing about this idea, as possible dangerous scenarios go through their head. Then we focus on the benefits for their learning and progress, considering what stops them stepping out and what they could do to address this. There are two groups of young people that are particularly cautious. Firstly, there are those young people who do not feel secure at home, as with one of my mentees, an only child, whose mother was away for a period caring for a sick relative but the school were not aware of this so she worried alone. As soon as Mum returned so did my mentee's smile and her can-do attitude. The other group is the very high achiever or perfectionist. Young people in this group often do not wish to risk their personal formula for success that allows them to stay in control. It takes quite some persuasion to get them to try anything new but if they do they soon see that this is ultimately the only way to get even better.

Case study 16

Rebecca (year 10) was extremely quietly spoken, so much so that I had to strain to hear what she was saying. We had already tackled a number of other barriers when she chose to focus on risk taking. I asked if there were any times she ever took risks. After some consideration she commented that she sometimes did at home when choosing what to draw or which medium to use. What made this possible I enquired? The key was that there was no time limit so if she messed it up she could stop and start again. At school this was not the case. I challenged her to try this in a small way at school. She identified that her current art project was in paint and colouring pencils so she decided to incorporate water colour pencils. This worked well and did not unnerve her. Each time she came we spent a few minutes thinking about what next. Risk-taking was now a possibility at school.

Case study 17

Georgia (year 12) looked in disbelief when I asked her about taking risks in her learning. However, when we came to choose her initial focus she very firmly selected this area. She had already identified that she was not good at asking questions in lessons generally as, in her opinion, other pupils asked 'good-sounding' questions and she saw hers as inferior. I assured her that her questions were almost certainly shared by other pupils who were not brave enough to voice them either. We agreed that she would ask a question in three lessons and note down what it felt like and what was the impact on her learning and that of others.

At our next session Georgia explained that she had decided to tackle her target by speaking to several teachers outside of the lesson. She could therefore not comment on how this affected others but it had helped her greatly and had not been nearly as scary as she expected. The information had been really useful in the January AS she had just taken.

Georgia than asked if it was ok to talk about outside issues. Of course it was. It transpired that she had been given a small role of responsibility but when she chose to make any decisions she was countered each time by an older person. We discussed a number of ideas and considered the possible outcomes. Eventually she decided she would be brave and tackle this issue with the person concerned. When I next saw her she was delighted to recount that the issue was no more. Addressing the concern straightaway had been the right strategy. I congratulated Georgia on applying her risk taking skills to other areas of life and explained that this was the point of our sessions, to equip her with resilience for life.

Following her initial steps of success, Georgia gained confidence to ask questions in class when the teacher invited them to do so. This enabled her to better understand her studies as at this point the answer was explained in a different way. She also spoke more regularly to teachers outside of class and ultimately, having been on a high level residential course relating to one of her A levels, became confident enough to share her new learning in class and to fully engage with class learning.

Case study 18
Jack (year 13) had obtained a place at Oxford. He worked hard and always achieved highly. I was keen to help him maintain his motivation and better equip him to cope with the transition to university where everyone would be as clever as him. I suggested he find something to take him out of his comfort zone. He decided he would produce a play with several secondary school contacts, which would make it separate to his college studies. He talked to his former secondary school and they were very happy to assign a rehearsal day and provide supervision thus ensuring commitment by the players. The play would be part of their art festival. They were delighted to welcome back their former pupils. Jack and his group created a theatre piece, which was very well received at the festival. Jack found balancing the time constraints and being the producer whilst completing his studies challenging yet rewarding. It stood him in very good stead for his time at Oxford.

I see mistakes as learning opportunities

Over time I have found that this question provokes a variety of responses in mentees. This ranges from enjoyment to embarrassment, frustration, guilt and anger. Some mentees are unable to move forwards. It is a good gauge of their resilience as a learner. Interestingly, the younger pupils are more likely to score themselves low. Perhaps because they see themselves as less able to address this situation, some not finding it easy to spot mistakes or maybe because lower down the school it is easier to be 'right' a lot of the time so when mistakes are made they are sometimes not able to accept they are fallible. This is worse in subjects where their perception is that everyone else is succeeding. One mentee explained that when she made a mistake she felt like she was letting someone down. In a more extreme case, a mentee told me that in year 8 he had got 99% for a test as he had missed out a letter in a French test and this still bugged him in year 10. I usually find that once we have talked about mistakes and learning, mentees quickly begin to adopt a more positive outlook.

Once pupils have successfully coped with the transition to sixth form they become much more positive about mistakes and it is generally those who have never had occasion to experience this who still struggle.

Case study 19
Callum (year 10) was generally very laid back about schoolwork and seemed almost distanced from it in conversation. I suspected that he hoped that if he blocked out any concerns then they would go away. However, when it came to extra-curricular activities he was more forthcoming. He was learning to play the piano and admitted that he often made mistakes when practising, which really frustrated him. If he played a wrong note then the next one was wrong too as his hand was in the wrong place. I wondered what he did then. As so often happens, he started again from the beginning even if he was a long way into the piece. We discussed the idea of concentrating on the phrase or interval where the mistake occurred and then playing the section around this phrase, asking the teacher for improvement strategies and also ensuring some days he just played the parts he knew well so that he maintained his enjoyment.

Callum tried these ideas and also thought of some of his own such as playing really slowly and gradually increasing his speed as he was able and spending longer perfecting his single-handed playing. As we moved on in mentoring sessions to other areas he was now better able to pinpoint why issues happened and what he could do to address them. He had understood the concept that lessons learnt in one area can be beneficially transferred to another.

Case study 20

Our son Noel struggled with mistakes. He had always done really well so much so that if he did make a mistake classmates were quick to notice and comment. He felt guilty and ashamed. We found that the best strategy was to talk him through these experiences and help him to learn from them. We also found that really supportive teachers were wonderful in addressing any unusual personal learning blocks he had in certain subjects such as long division in maths. The area where he most needed help though was after modules or exams. Sometimes, when he returned home, he shouted 'that was rubbish!'

'So you have failed then?' I countered.

'Oh no! Six of the seven questions were ok' he assured me.

'So you have lost the marks for one question. How many marks was it worth?' I enquired.

'Ten but I could do most of it' he explained.

'Ok, so you have lost three marks?' I wondered.

'Yes.'

'Well then that will not affect your final grade so I would not worry too much.'

This pattern happened regularly after exams but was an essential exercise to allow him to voice his anxiety and then move on and concentrate on the next exam.

Each time I have told this story to parents they laugh knowingly. It is a common occurrence. I have also shared it with mentees to encourage them to keep going and assure them that making mistakes is quite normal and in fact an extremely good way to learn.

Case study 21

Amy (year 13) was waiting for me outside the mentoring room, as white as a sheet. She had contacted me to see if we could have a shorter session, 30 minutes and then to see if just 5 or 10 minutes was possible. I showed her in and asked her to tell me what was worrying her. She had just had an unexpected chemistry test that was very hard, the marks of which would count towards her A level and no feedback would be given. She was extremely concerned.

I already knew from previous conversations that mistakes caused her to panic. She usually told her mum and then blocked out her worry without allowing time to discuss possible future solutions. This she told me was a family trait.

We spent 35 minutes talking generally and I assured her that teachers wanted their students to do well so I thought she needed to talk to the teacher and tell him how she felt. I was sure there was a positive way forward.

Next time Amy came to see me she was much more smiley and relaxed. She had got ten out of fifteen for her chemistry test. She had spoken to the teacher who, although he had expected her to do better, was shocked to hear that Amy had thought she had done really badly. He had explained that there would be a chance in the future to do another one and then submit the best grade. Amy, it seemed, had got the test totally out of perspective.

From that time onwards Amy began to accept that she could turn mistakes and anxiety into a positive. She started her revision earlier, tried to learn from mistakes and looked at ways to tackle those areas she knew were potential pitfalls.

Case study 22
Joseph was in year 13. We had a long discussion unpicking his learning. He confided that when he first started in sixth form he had found learning difficult and felt guilty but told no-one. He did the same with mistakes. When I enquired how his family dealt with difficulties and mistakes he said he did not know as they did not talk about such things. In our sessions he greatly enjoyed the opportunity to analyse his performance and look for the best way for him to improve. Over time he became more open to new ways of doing things, spoke to his teacher for advice and started to talk to his parents as well.

I never feel stressed or pressurised

Many mentees state that they suffer from pressure and stress. The most common causes are coursework, exams, constant reference to revision and exams, expectations of others and of self, perfectionism, inability to understand something despite much effort and lots of commitments. Many do not choose to focus on stress as such but rather the areas causing it and in so doing ultimately remedy the stress. However, there are some for whom the level of stress is such that we have to tackle it head on.

It is also important to note that for a small number of young people stress is what they call the adrenaline rush they get during the build-up to exams and as long as this is a short-term experience, it aids their performance. One year 13 boy told me that in the revision period he read and re-read his text books, often for four hours at a time, getting quicker each time. As he did so, he linked the content in his head. By the time the exams arrived he had a very clear mind map of the whole topic. During this period he did not sleep or eat well but his mental capacity remained unimpaired. He gained a place at Oxford. My advice to him was not to engage in such activity for too long, as he may think necessary in a highly intellectual environment. He has since informed me that he still uses his method to good effect but has now built in a number of fun activities as well.

Case study 23

Jordan (year 10) was a high achieving mentee. He operated in a constant state of stress. What were the main triggers I asked? He listed course assessments (four pieces in two days), exams, being regularly told to revise, parental expectation, lots of Young Chamber where he was a named officer and doing homework until 11pm. Where to start?

Jordan chose to focus on organisation, homework, deadlines and time management. We started to unpick this. He explained that he left all his homework to the night before, including long-term pieces. Sometimes he had to give in homework unfinished as it was so late that his Mum had insisted he go to bed. The trouble was he took so long to do it as he became easily distracted. To my amazement he estimated distractions accounted for 2–3 hours every night! Anything caused a distraction: PS3, TV, food, tidying his room, Facebook. We decided that the key would be to manage distractions and to plan a schedule. He undertook to draw up one before our next session which I suggested should include relaxation and social activities. It would also be a good idea to consult his Mum about any family events. I advised that big pieces of work should be broken down into sections.

With regard to the distractions he felt that this would require will power. He could turn off his PS3. It was the laptop that was the major problem, his use of bookmarks meant that distraction was only a click away. He would remove the bookmark bar.

I looked forward to the update at the next session. Jordan told me he now had a timetable on the cork board by his bed, complete with a homework column, spacing it across the week. He also had a reserve or emergency column that allowed for any unexpected homework or event. He was now doing his homework at his allotted time, generally as soon as it was set. It was always in on time and his grades were up. It also took much less time as he had cut the distractions, only listening to music through his phone, not his laptop and the bookmarks bar was no more. His stress levels had decreased. The only thing he worried about now was whether he had remembered to put it in his bag! His mum was delighted as she no longer had to nag him to do his work or to turn out the light. Jordan himself found that he now had much more time to use as he wished and sometimes even had a completely free evening.

By the next session his maths teacher had made a point of commenting on the transformation he had seen. Homework was now done very well and in on time. Jordan was able to explain that this was due to mentoring. Later in the term, he also told me that fellow members at Young Chamber had asked him if he had less homework. Previously he had often left meetings early to go and do his homework. However, his level of distractions had not meant that this early departure had helped much. Now, with no decrease in his homework schedule, he was able to stay for the complete meeting, in a more focussed state whilst still keeping up with his work, doing it to a better standard. What a big effect such small changes had made!

Case study 24

Anna (year 10) chose to address stress and pressure. She identified that this was only an issue at school. Initially we focussed on lack of understanding in Spanish (see 'What are your weaknesses?'). Anna then moved on to talk about her lack of confidence in RE. Using a technique that my youngest son's teacher had employed to build his confidence at KS2 SATS, I asked her to produce a mind map of all she knew, thinking through all the connections. This really grabbed her attention, especially the possibility of using colours for clarity. It was sure to be a work of art. She would display it on her bedroom wall and bring me a photo next time. Anna quickly realised just how much she actually knew. Her confidence grew. At the next parents' evening the RE teacher was delighted to report that Anna had become more vocal.

Anna then unpicked her anxiety in science. She worried about answering questions in class in case she got it wrong and looked silly. I encouraged her to answer even if she was unsure and tell me how it went and how she felt. At the next session she excitedly informed me that instead of feeling silly she had actually learnt a lot. The teacher had said that her answer was not quite right and had explained why not. She would definitely do this again as she found she had learnt it better through having initially got it wrong.

Case study 25
Lucy (year 10) was predicted to achieve A* in all her subjects. She thought very deeply and always spent a lot of time and effort on her work. What she lacked though was the ability to relax. I was concerned that ultimately she would burn out. We began to talk about what she liked to do in her free time. She was very keen on fresh air; going for walks or cycle rides. We looked together online at weekend or half-term events and courses run by the local park. She decided to go along occasionally with a friend.

Lucy also enjoyed drawing. All her GCSEs were academic. So, I suggested that she spent time drawing. She wanted this to be purposeful, so chose to draw characters or objects from historical periods that interested her but that were not on the curriculum. Lucy started to draw every day and each time she finished a drawing brought it along to show me. At my encouragement she also showed them to the history teacher, which lead to occasional opportunities for some really interesting conversations and a request that she help to man the history section at GCSE choice evening to enthuse prospective historians.

Science was Lucy's other fascination. She subscribed to the BBC Wildlife Magazine. When I set her target at the end of one session I asked her to come along and enthuse me about something she had read in her magazine. The next time she told me all about the possible reintroduction of the lynx in Scotland. Her enthusiasm and interest were tangible. Afterwards she commented how lovely it was to have the opportunity to talk about non-curriculum material. It made the rest of her learning seem so much more meaningful and she particularly appreciated the fact that she could choose what to read.

Case study 26

'I feel like I am working all the time!' Bethany (year 12) responded to my 'How are you today?'

'That sounds exhausting,' I replied. 'Talk me through how you spend your day.'

Bethany was a conscientious student who always met deadlines, producing high-quality work. She also had a large number of extra-curricular commitments, a Saturday job, was learning to drive, was trying to decide what to study at university and was aiming to take the EPQ (Extended Project Qualification). In addition she spent time supporting a number of friends and often offered to help at school events. I had a few other similar mentees.

We talked about how much homework she got and when she fitted it in and her commitments schedule. Bethany was making very good use of down-time, filling occasional frees with homework, so much so that she never needed to take her maths home. Her busyness also meant that study sessions were highly focussed but she needed a regular, long uninterrupted space to complete her artwork. It took quite a while noting down all the details and listening to the anecdotes surrounding each subject or activity. I suggested I take away the 'problem' and see if I could make everything fit.

Before the next session I played with all the different parts. There were not enough hours in a week! I needed to be creative. At the following session I asked a few further questions. Would the list be the same in year 13? Did all these activities need to happen now? When was the latest date she would like to achieve them? Where did she find time to socialise or have fun?

In so doing I discovered that Bethany intended to keep all four subjects in year 13. This being the case, I asked her to consider carefully whether she needed to do the EPQ or would have time to do it justice. Some of the commitments, such as music lessons could perhaps happen every two weeks, thus freeing up a good amount of space due to lesson time and travel each way. Choosing a university subject could be spread across the next six or nine months. I suggested she order prospectuses from the top universities and carry them around one at a time, allowing her to dip into them whenever a few minutes arose, just concentrating on the subject offer. She could then allocate a day in the holidays to summarise her findings. She could also plan a trip to a local university offering many courses, which would allow her to go to a range of talks and make it easier to decide which courses appealed. After this she could concentrate on looking at subject rankings and university facilities in general. As for driving lessons, she could perhaps focus these in the summer holiday or space them out so that they became a form of relaxation.

Before I could continue, Bethany told me that she had also been thinking and talking to friends who had suggested she say 'no' more often. This, I agreed, was a wonderful idea. She did not need to be unkind but she did need to limit herself. If she worked out how much time she needed to spend on her work, week by week and made sure she blocked out this amount, then it would be much easier to say no. I also insisted that she plan in some fun at least once a week, even if it was watching her favourite TV programme, playing a game with her family or going for a walk or a coffee.

The next time I saw Bethany, her smile had returned. She was now in control of her work and life, it was no longer controlling her.

I am a perfectionist

Perfectionism is a trait that many of my mentees tell me they definitely possess, with a small number scoring noncommittally and only a couple saying they definitely do not. They have extremely high expectations of themselves. This is often something that they have acquired from experience, as they have regularly done very well and now expect this to happen. Low or slow performance does not match their self-image. This is often reinforced by the expectation of others. Perfectionism also describes a characteristic way of working of certain pupils who drive themselves to produce a perfect piece of work, settling for nothing less.

I ask those who declare themselves to be perfectionists whether they see this as a positive or a negative trait. They generally tell me it is both. Positive aspects cited are determination to get things right, perseverance to keep going until they 'get it', producing excellent work, having good, high aspirations and the drive to do well. Negative aspects are getting frustrated with little things, getting annoyed if they cannot 'get it', feeling compelled to be constantly meticulous, writing too much and taking a very long time to complete work (this is especially true of art and DT students). One insightful mentee told me that he is a perfectionist when things are going well but he is quick to give up if they do not work out. So often this is the reaction of gifted pupils, they cannot accept struggle or 'failure'. Our son Noel regularly threw his books across the dining room when doing his English homework, he found the blank white page so daunting. At other times he put himself under intense pressure to perform at the highest level. Sadly I have some mentees who have shut the door on certain subjects or options as they cannot get beyond the struggle stage. Many address their perfectionism by discussing and tackling the effects such as stress, inability to cope with mistakes, to keep going when stuck, risk aversion and difficulty in asking teachers for help or in group working. Please see these sections for their stories.

The minority of mentees who definitely do not see themselves as perfectionist often have low self-esteem or are unable to believe that they can succeed. It is certainly worth exploring these possibilities with them.

Case study 27

Jordan (year 10) whose story is featured under 'stress' was a classic perfectionist, very hard on himself if he did not do as well as he thought he should. He particularly excelled at maths, business and IT, all of which he very much enjoyed. However, he told me he was not a perfectionist in languages as he did not enjoy them so much but that his teachers had high expectations. I encouraged him to concentrate on stimulating enjoyment rather than top results. One idea was to be more creative in his written work, something he found difficult.

At his next session he told me that he was enjoying German more now as he knew more of the vocabulary. Probing deeper, I discovered, that in fact what he did not like, was the feeling of not knowing. I suggested he start to look at the German news on-line once a week so that he became more used to the feeling of being out of his depth and thus less unnerved by it. We also decided to look for ways of giving him more experience of not being top or right. He identified business as a useful subject in this respect as, when working in a group, lots could go wrong and did and he was working on learning to cope with this. In IT he was designing a web-page and the more he learnt the more he wanted to alter it but he had realised that it was important to learn when to stop. His positive perception increased his coping ability even further.

Case study 28

Emma (year 13) was a very hard-working student. She gave herself a 5 for perfectionism and told me that she tended to beat herself up too much when she could not do things and over-stressed trying to make things really good. I asked her to talk me through what this looked like. Emma explained that she came from a family who were excessively tidy. For her part she was not. However, when it came to work she spent huge amounts of time on chemistry homework in a bid to make it as good as possible. I told her that my youngest daughter had done the same in English literature and had exhausted herself. She could totally understand. She was often very tired after late nights and her Mum was always nagging her to stop. My daughter had eventually followed the advice of her aunt and set herself a time limit, stopping her essay writing at the end of it and submitting it as it was. To her amazement, she had got virtually the same mark as she used to when she worked very late. This altered her working pattern. I wondered if Emma thought her excessive effort achieved a significantly higher result or if a little less effort would be almost as effective but significantly less exhausting, leaving her more time for other things. Emma was intrigued.

At our next session she told me that she had set time limits for all her work. Her Mum had also said that she needed to have some free time. So now she started earlier and was able to have time off later. She continued to achieve highly.

Case study 29

Katie (year 13) was a driven student. She aspired to be a doctor and saw it as essential to always perform well. Her strength was that she was always ahead of the game. She worked excessively hard and prepared minutely for every test and exam, going through every possible question. I suggested this could also be a weakness. This stopped her in her tracks. I wondered how she would cope in an emergency with the unexpected. Had she developed the necessary skills? Katie thought very hard. Her family always planned everything to the very last detail. She went away to find opportunities to address this.

Case study 30

Several of my mentees have taken art or product design at A level. For all of them the issue has been time. One mentee told me 'I am aiming for amazing, but I need to juggle the rest of my life'. Inspiration and ideas have rarely been a problem it is the deadlines that are. This can cause huge anxiety. Some tell me they are always creating, others spend hours late at night on their art, struggling to fit it in around the high demands of their other subjects, which mean that ironically they sometimes spend less time on the art when this is their chosen future path, some push deadlines to the limit. What is the answer?

Solutions are varied. Some set aside a whole day at a weekend, so that they can take as long as they like. Others take on board the need to plan time for art as with other subjects and if necessary to speak to those other subject teachers who set large amounts of work. A number have realised, eventually, that to aim for absolutely amazing will ultimately be too time consuming, so have negotiated with their teacher how far they can go towards their ideals whilst still remaining within the allotted time. At times this includes staying after school, coming in on TD days or working at lunch. It is important they feel they have been able to show their potential and produce a final piece of which they can be proud. However, learning to respect time constraints and to balance competing demands is also vital.

I am sensitive

Some gifted young people are highly sensitive; some find change particularly difficult, some have a heightened sense of justice, others are strongly affected by different types of voices, and others have an exaggerated ability to worry about what may happen in the future. In all of these cases, the availability of a non-dismissive, listening ear is extremely helpful as well as someone to provide reassurance and, if necessary, a way forward. Interestingly, year 13 seems to be when mentees are particularly likely to score themselves highly in terms of sensitivity.

Occasionally the sensitivity becomes extreme, anxiety builds and can lead the pupil into clinical anxiety or depression. I have experienced this first hand with my own son and also had the opportunity to help another mentee through this state. It is essential that pupils seek medical attention either in the form of medication or counselling. During this period a mentor can help greatly by providing a ready and safe listening space. Thereafter, it is particularly helpful to encourage the pupil to regularly talk through particular anxieties of the moment.

Case study 31
Connor (year 12) was highly reactive to criticism and did not like doing badly in tests. He had worked hard for his GCSEs and continued to do so in the sixth form. However, when he got his results for his first science tests he was horrified to find that he had gained a D in one subject and an E in the other. He felt very low. He told me that he had found the tests hard and realised that he had only known about half of each question, had made some stupid mistakes and after the first question had panicked. I asked him how this compared to the rest of the class. No-one had fared well and many had achieved even lower grades. We talked about how to learn and improve from this. He did not seem reassured.

Was there anything else bothering him I wondered? Connor explained that one teacher had reassured the class, went over the mistakes and was very helpful. However, the other teacher had immediately called home to speak to his mother. He had found this humiliating. I assured him that the teacher was doing what she thought best but suggested that he talk to her so that she knew how he was feeling. This he agreed to do. By the next session he was much happier. The teacher had reassured him that the key was his exam technique and indeed in the next test he had done much better. He had successfully moved on from his anxiety.

Case study 32

As Ryan (year 10) came into the room I noticed that he was shaking. This he continued to do throughout the entire session. He completed the questionnaire, giving himself a three for sensitivity. At the end, in response to the question 'What would you like to gain from the sessions?' he told me that he wanted to find a way to stop being in trouble at school. He then explained at length that his behaviour used to be poor but had improved. However, he still got blamed for things which were not his fault and got his name on the board. This did not seem to happen to other people. Some of the clever pupils in his class called out and yet they were not reprimanded. When he pointed out the inconsistencies to his teacher he was in even more trouble and ended up with a detention. We discussed what he could do to improve and what he should do if he thought things were unfair.

Over the next few sessions we returned to our discussion and I noticed that the shaking gradually stopped. Keen to find a positive way forward I commended him on his appreciation of justice. I told him about my son Noel. I explained that when Noel was eight, he had noticed some boys being unkind to another boy and had gone to speak to them. When they took no notice he had pushed one of them. At this point the teacher spotted him and Noel was in trouble. The other boys blended into the crowd. He was indignant at the injustice. We praised his good intentions but explained why there was a process to follow. It took him a while to accept that it was not a good idea to be an avenging angel at school. It was better to inform a teacher and allow them to sort it out.

I told Ryan that a heightened sense of justice was sometimes a characteristic of a gifted pupil and should be used to good effect. He was not part of the school council and did not think it was cool to speak out on behalf of good causes or 'bake cakes' to raise money. We spent several sessions looking at charity web-sites until he found a cause in which he believed and which offered a sponsored activity he felt suited his image.

Co-incidentally he was taught by my link teacher several times a week. I shared his concerns with her. She was also able to tap into his sense of justice and if ever he became too loud in class had only to tell him that he was not being fair to his classmates and immediately the situation was resolved.

I am confident

Relatively few mentees score themselves extremely low on confidence but quite a number give themselves a three. It is interesting therefore that confidence is one of the most common areas on which mentees choose to focus. It is useful to explore what they see as the necessary attributes of the confident pupil. Key characteristics seem to be the ability to speak in front of an audience, to ask or answer questions in class and to talk to teachers. Their levels of confidence are also, in their minds, closely related to their achievement. Confidence certainly grows with maturity and I find that the year 13 mentees often score themselves more highly.

Many mentees also address a lack of confidence by tackling other areas and their stories can be found throughout this book.

Case study 33

Shannon (year 10), a highly reflective mentee, told me that she had always lacked confidence. She did not like speaking in front of the class as she was afraid of sounding silly. In group work she felt left out. I suggested we concentrate on improving in one subject. She chose drama. Her ambitious target was to contribute to class discussions five times over two lessons. She would come up with an idea and be confident in voicing it. I asked her to note the effect her contributions had on class learning and to rate how she felt.

At the next session she reported that she had managed to contribute three times. She had been fascinated to see how other people had reacted and how her thoughts had caused other ideas to spark. She had not been afraid. She had also actively participated in an inter-school discussion event and gave me valuable feedback that if pupils were first given time to share their ideas to check they were not alone then many more would contribute.

Several sessions later, Shannon commented that she no longer saw herself as lacking in confidence. Her perception, she said, had changed as she had realised that, in her own way, she was confident and this realisation, in turn, positively affected her performance. I congratulated her on her unique contributions and encouraged her to continue thinking deeply and sharing her insights for the benefit of all. We researched ways that she could access high level debate on some of the topics in which she was interested. The 'avaaz' website proved ideal. She also talked to my link teacher about the possibility of starting a debating society.

Case study 34

Rebecca (year 10) was incredibly shy. She was determined to learn to speak in front of an audience. Her main goal was to ask questions in class. It was very evident that we needed to tackle this aim step by step. We decided to start by speaking to one teacher out of class. I asked her to notice what it felt like and how it impacted on her learning.

At the next session she told me that she had spoken to her teacher at the end of class to discuss how to take her coursework forward. Although nervous beforehand, she had felt ok and the teacher's ideas were very helpful. We kept the same target. This time her questioning prompted the teacher to show her a new technique to use in her work. She rated the scariness of the experience as 3–4 out of 10. She would now seek out a different teacher. We then moved onto taking risks in learning.

Gradually, as she learnt from both targets, Rebecca became a more confidant speaker and one day told me she had asked the maths teacher to explain a concept in class and also told me she had asked someone she did not know for assistance at a family social she attended. Her confidence grew.

Case study 35

Emma (year 13) was lacking in confidence when it came to answering questions in class. Much of this stemmed from some unpleasant experiences long ago in primary school. In discussion it was evident that she thought very deeply and that her contributions would benefit her fellow students enormously. She told me that she often thought so hard that she second guessed herself and convinced herself that she was wrong. She was also discouraged from participating by the very smart people who got the answer quickly and the intricate thought processes of one lad in her class. She found this very intimidating. What she really wanted to know was the 'why?'

We talked at length about the value of deep thought, noting that speed did not necessarily mean other students were more clever than her and that different contributions help different people. She reflected and remarked that when she was working with her friends out of class, their wondering questions acted as a springboard for their learning. It was also the same when she was watching television. She often sub-consciously made links between new knowledge and other areas of her learning. She agreed to ask some 'whys' in maths. From then onwards she felt comfortable talking to the teacher and enjoyed asking questions in class. This new skill also enabled her to discuss with confidence at her university interview. She told me the experience was like two colleagues chatting about a subject about which they were both passionate. At the end of our sessions she commented how valuable it had been to have a mentor with whom she could talk to help her build her confidence.

Case study 36

Claire (year 11) wanted to improve her confidence in French. We decided to see if she could raise her hand more in class, at least three times a lesson. At the next session we reflected how this had felt and she admitted it was not nearly as scary as she had expected. Our next target was for her to use her French when she went on the art trip to Paris. On her return she told me that she had spoken a lot as hardly any of the others had been confident enough to do so and many were not doing languages so she was their mouthpiece. She thought it was really cool to be able to be understood abroad. She ultimately changed her A Level choices and took French, achieving an A.

Case study 37

Emily (year 10) lacked confidence in maths. She struggled to understand the concepts. We discussed the way forward and she decided to do some exercises from her text book and see if the teacher would mark them. He was delighted to do so. She found the exercises easier than she had expected.

She realised that she needed to be more pro-active and independent and now wondered how to do that in science as the teaching was generally from the front. We thought about all the different things she could do. One topic she was particularly finding difficult was genes. As I mentored several pupils at the school, I was able to match her up with an older pupil studying biology at A level. This was mutually beneficial. Emily found her peer mentor explained in simpler terms and the sixth former found the exercise made her explanations more concise. We also looked at physics, which was her least favourite science, and I asked her to research three more facts about her current topic but not on the internet (so she had to consider different forms of research) and to pose herself a wondering question.

Emily considered static electricity and created a lovely visual piece. She wondered why a balloon when rubbed against her jumper to create static, stuck to the wall instead of falling off due to gravitational force. This provided her with a wonderful opportunity to talk to her teacher and show him her independent learning. I also asked her to write up her learning experience for the school magazine. Emily greatly enjoyed this target. In fact the following year, when considering her A level options, she actively considered taking physics! Emily now had confidence to talk to teachers when she needed help with her learning, or to independently go forwards instead of struggling alone.

Case study 38

Upon reflection Luke (year 10) thought that his lack of confidence was limiting his progress. It meant he did not take risks, ask questions, talk to teachers and he found it difficult to listen and learn at the same time. He realised that it was up to him to take some personal steps. We set a target for him to ask a 'big question' in one of his subjects either in class or out.

At our next session he mentioned that he had decided to talk to his physics teacher out of class as he was 'pretty curious' about a comment the teacher had made during the lesson. He described how they had made a chain and let electricity pass through them. The teacher had said that the current was more dangerous than the voltage. Why would that be? Now he knew, he told me wryly, that was why you should not jam your fingers into a socket.

We next considered risk taking. He told me that in maths, if there was a question on the board that he did not understand, he asked his mates before he tried it himself. He decided that he was prepared to have a go at it using his own initiative and risk getting it wrong, after all if he became too anxious he could always use the computer package 'My Maths'. He started to do so. He still got lost at times and had to ask for help but his perseverance grew. As a by-product he found his maths knowledge grew so that he was able to copy down from the board more quickly, leaving him time to follow class discussion.

Luke received a very low mark for a science mock as the format had changed. He, in common with the rest of his class, realised that they had to apply themselves independently to the learning taking place. Luke's confidence had been hit but he now knew that to ask questions would help enormously. He bought a more detailed revision guide and made the most of any additional revision sessions offered. He also made a science revision plan on his ipod of 90 minutes a night, with 30 minutes on each science area and each one divided into three subjects. In our sessions we looked at a range of university courses, exploring the grade requirements, this gave him a focus.

Luke considered that his confidence levels had gone from a 5 to a 7. Increased revision had helped and he was answering questions independently and getting them right so he would answer even more. He noticed that he was worrying less as he had realised that he could change things to how he liked them. He was now an active partner in his own learning.

Case study 39

William (year 13) was highly confident in terms of work, with a rigorous and highly focussed study method and a fascination for learning that had achieved him a place at Oxford. However, now that he was no longer doing drama (as at GCSE) but purely academic subjects, he was finding it increasingly difficult to talk to new adults. Drama had given him that confidence. We talked for quite some time about this. It was evident that at university he would come across many new people and it would certainly be advantageous if he could speak to them easily. Would it be possible for him to take part in any remaining school productions? He felt this could limit his study time but agreed to help back stage with some of the lower school productions at least in the final weeks. We still needed to find another solution to build confidence.

When prospective new teachers came to the school on interview, I wondered, who showed them around? William was unsure. As a member of the sixth form who had been there since year 7 he surely knew the school well. Would he feel able to offer his services? With his agreement, I contacted my link teacher to suggest this idea. She was very keen. As with any new idea, it took a while for it to be fully accepted and embedded but by the following year some of my less confidant year 13s were reaping the benefit.

Teachers often praise my learning

This question formed part of a survey I put together long ago to investigate the experience of the gifted and talented children at the primary school where I was a governor. Some told me that they did not often receive praise as they were expected to do well. It was the weaker or more badly behaved children who got the most praise whenever they produced particularly good work.

I have decided to include this question as praise definitely impacts on a pupil's well-being. Interestingly, many of the older pupils have told me that praise is not something you expect post-16. However, it is clear that when they do receive it, in whatever form, as long as it is not overdone, they are delighted and it certainly helps build confidence, perseverance and resilience. I have found that the comments this statement raises have produced valuable insights for my link teachers on perception and impact. There is some correlation between the pupil who is very quiet or does not talk to teachers and low levels of praise.

Case study 40

Harry (year 10) was a very bubbly, personable, chatty lad. In response to this statement he said he was more likely to be told off. Why was this? He loved to talk. Instead of reprimanding him I enquired what he was talking about. It seemed he had never been asked this question before. Was he talking about the football the previous night, Britain's Got Talent or about his learning? He admitted that he was sometimes 'just talking' so I asked him to consider how this made the teacher and quite likely some of the other pupils feel. However, most of the time he was talking about the learning as this was how he learnt best. He would either be sharing his ideas with someone else or asking them for clarification. I wondered if the teacher actually knew what he was talking about. We set a target for him to go and speak to his maths teacher, to apologise for any disruption and to ask if he could be allowed to talk when necessary in the lesson. She was delighted to hear his explanation and immediately started to incorporate 'learning talk' into her lessons, benefitting several other pupils and allowing Harry to receive praise for his learning insights.

I cope well with exams

Over the years I have become increasingly aware that a small number of gifted young people have a virtual phobia of exams that cumulatively impacts ever more negatively on performance. They rarely share their experiences with their teachers and so suffer in silence, accepting this as their lot and not considering there could be a solution. Schools do not always see the repeating patterns as subjects are looked at individually and low performance, if noted, is often put down to an off day. Quite often these patterns only occur in the final years of study. Future destination and performance may well be negatively affected. Expert help is available when the pupils are identified.

Many mentoring conversations have centred on the difficulty mentees find in exam preparation. Gifted pupils often find tests in the early years of secondary school relatively easy and regularly achievable without revision. For many this is also true of GCSEs, what one of my son's teachers referred to as 'A walk in the park.' Some feel restrained by the recommended school revision methods. One mentee told me that she felt liberated when she heard that it was acceptable to just revise what you knew you needed to revise, instead of dutifully trudging through the whole syllabus.

The real issues seem to arise in sixth form when studies are more challenging and independent and some revision is essential. Many mentees are at a loss how to tackle this. Others feel guilty that they are unable to succeed without revising. Once performance has dipped below previous levels, some then assume they are now unable to do any better, or begin to doubt the efficacy of continued effort. Mentoring sessions need to concentrate on enabling mentees to stop being a victim and to find individual strategies for progress and success. Others are floored by the vagaries of exam board marking and need support to get back on track. (See Charlotte's story, case study 11.)

I have had some fascinating conversations with mentees about how to plan their revision schedule based on what they need to revise, what methods suit them best and how to fit their revision into their personal schedule without cancelling the rest of their life. Very few have opted for the traditional approach: work for one hour, have a short break, work for another hour. They have come up with lots of creative ideas including a pick and mix routine where they list all the things to be revised, choose how many they need to achieve in a week and then revise according to how they feel each day whilst still keeping an eye on exam dates. They tell me these sessions are invaluable.

Case study 41

Ben (year 10) told me from the very beginning that he was a B pupil and was unable to achieve any higher. He particularly found exams stressful and achieved less well than in class when he felt more relaxed and less rushed. In exams he was always writing until the last minute and worried that he would not finish in time. For his first target I suggested he try doing past papers to time at home. The idea, I explained, was not to feel guilty for not finishing but to get used to how this period of time felt. He should work for this amount of time, note how much he had done and then complete the other questions. As he became accustomed to the feeling of time he would also become better able to manage it. In his next exam he reported he was not too nervous and therefore found his performance improved. Practicing working to time had really helped. He achieved a higher grade.

Later in the year he reported that he was floundering again and assumed it must again be timing. There was a distinct difference between his class and his exam performance. I wondered if he did anything differently in each situation. He then told me that in class he worked through the paper in order but in exams, wanting to maximise his marks, he did the questions with the highest marks first. This was increasing his stress, instead of allowing him to work up to the hardest questions and so was counter-productive. I praised his effort to find the best strategy and suggested he maintain the method he used to good effect in class. The strategy worked. He achieved his A.

Case study 42

Our son Noel spoke French very well. He prepared assiduously for his spoken exam, practising spontaneous speaking. Before he left for school on the exam day we had half an hour's practice. He was stunning. I was shocked therefore when he returned home to hear that it had not gone well. Not long into the exam his mind had gone blank. From then onwards he had only been able to use the most basic of phrases. We realised that to avoid this in future exams he needed to have some fall back phrases at the ready which would give him a few moments grace to regain his thoughts. This realisation proved invaluable for him and has also helped many other mentees with whom I have discussed strategies for exam 'freeze', allowing them to dismiss the adrenaline freezing their brain and to complete their task. As one of my daughter's teachers told her at KS2 SATS, 'celebrate with the examiner what you do know, do not dwell on what you do not'.

Case study 43

Amy (year 13) struggled with exam nerves. This had not been a problem at GCSE as she was confident in her learning. Even if this had not been the case though, she would not have spoken to the teachers as she was too shy, she admitted. Now she was working on overload. She was doing some retakes as well as her A2 exams as she was aiming for a high level university. She felt under great pressure.

We talked about how she coped with stress during the exam period. At home she countered stress when revising by thinking about her holidays, or going for a walk or a run. In the exam room she read through the questions, which sometimes helped and sometimes it did not. Much has been written about maximising exam performance and I was able to share with her the ideas in *The study skills handbook* by Stella Cottrell. She decided to try the 'I can' technique, giving herself positive messages both outside the exam room and during the exam. I asked her to use this in her January exams and to report back how it went. When I next saw her she was more relaxed. The exams had seemed easier she felt. The relaxation tip had definitely helped. We repeated the process for the summer series and also looked at tips for improving her recall of various maths processes. She greatly enjoyed this analytical approach.

Case study 44

Laura (year 13) was the first person in her family to study in the sixth form or to be considering university. Her GCSE grades had suggested she would achieve highly at A levels but this was not the case and she was becoming demoralised. We discussed her methodology. She wrote out her notes to aid recall and had made a series of key cards and mind maps. She had also been given a revision pack. However, she had never tried a revision timetable. We talked through what she needed to do, how she would like to do it and how many times and how long each step would take. She then chose to fit this into her diary during our session, working backwards from each exam date and ensuring she did not overload any one day. She was delighted with the finished timetable and remarked that this would stop her worrying she had forgotten something. As part of this we considered writing some timed essays for some of her subjects, something she had never done but which teachers had said they would welcome. We also talked about doing practice papers, again something she had never tried out of class.

At our next session Laura reported that she was now making greater use of mind maps with lots of colour. These enabled her to make links between more of her learning and so she had a better understanding of the whole. She had also completed some practice essays and had them marked and done some practice papers, which had helped with structure and timing. She had consequently become more concise in her essay writing, which she was sure would help to raise her grades.

Laura had greatly benefitted from our sessions. She had become a partner in her own learning and had been given the opportunity to make the revision period her own.

Case study 45

Our youngest son Isaac did not appreciate how much extra work was needed to do well in languages at AS level. Despite a poor exam result he decided to continue at A2. His effort increased and so did his achievement levels. He retook all the AS exams in January of year 13 whilst also studying for his A2s and this time achieved a higher result. He was poised to do equally well in his A2 exams. However, as the exams loomed and his focus shifted to other subjects, he began to doubt his ability and lessen his effort in French. It became clear that he was querying the point. If he could not achieve an A was it worthwhile? We spent time pinpointing and addressing his weakest areas. I also encouraged him to speak to his teachers who were very pleased to support him. His confidence and self-belief returned. The highest grades were hard to achieve but it was always worth aiming high. The challenge and his struggle were highly beneficial in helping him to appreciate the messiness and difficulty of the process of learning and equipped him well for some of the seemingly insurmountable problems he would certainly face in university studies.

I am good at managing distractions

Gifted young people are just as prone to distractions as others. Distraction seems to have different causes in school and at home. In outstanding lessons pupils are fully engaged and in the flow. However, at other times, some find the behaviour of other group or class members can be an issue, particularly excessive talking when they are trying to concentrate. Others tell me that they are more distracted in lessons they do not like and these are often those they do not think they are good at. Some are distracted by teacher presentation or prolonged teaching.

At home distractions are manifold. Technology is cited the most but pupils are also distracted by eating, cake making, tidying their room and other family members. Some solutions are included in the chapters on homework and exams and Jordan's story under stress.

I ask mentees if they could wave a magic wand what would alter the situation. Thoughts are divided between personal action requiring will power and issues requiring school action such as the interest level or depth of teaching. One highly reflective mentee talked through her engagement level in each lesson. In some lessons, such as English, she talked to her neighbour who was very good at the subject so this was worthwhile. However, in some lessons she was engaged in idle chatter. She asked to change her seating position, to sit at the front. Learning improved vastly as it was now the teacher, the board and her. Several others decided to make notes to keep their focus, although this involved instruction in the art of note-taking. Over time a number have complained about being talked at by the teacher, which made long-term concentration difficult. These mentees, after considering anything they could do to personally improve the situation, have plucked up courage to talk to their teacher or maybe their tutor to suggest more visual content, interaction or challenge in lessons.

Mentees have decided to exercise great will power to manage distractions at home. This has stuck when they have discovered how much time is saved, allowing more free time and the positive impact on grades and family life. One told me he had adopted a new mantra 'Get rid of distractions and do homework straightaway'. This gave him lots of time for computer gaming. Another had Facebook only on his phone so that his computer now worked faster and distractions were cut and homework completed more swiftly. However, not all technology is bad. One year 13 told me he used Skype and Facebook. This did hinder his rate of progress but learning with others helped his understanding. Following our conversation he was now much less distracted by random links.

Case study 46

Chris (year 9) told me he would like to understand why he always got distracted. This had been the case since primary school. I asked him if he was the boy who always quickly completed tasks set during carpet time and then got into trouble for fiddling or chatting. He was amazed. How did I know? We investigated several of the statements on the questionnaire. Ultimately we concluded that he was not being challenged, engaged or inspired by the learning taking place. This led to teachers telling him off for lack of concentration. He had fairly low self-esteem. This did not make him bad but in need of some strategies to ensure maximum engagement and interest. We constructed a mind map with strategies for a wide range of eventualities. This was also copied to the G and T co-ordinator.

Chris' mind map

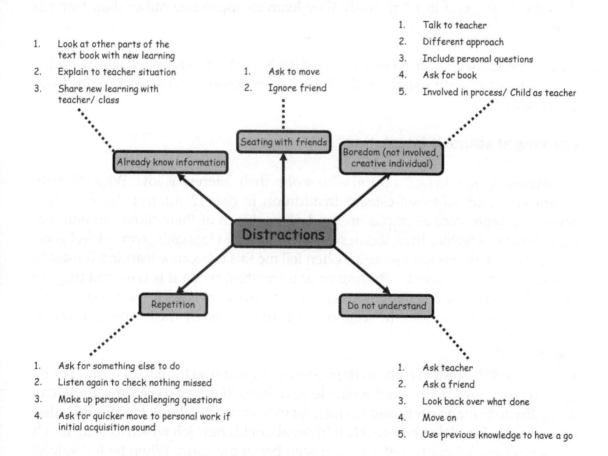

1. Look at other parts of the text book with new learning
2. Explain to teacher situation
3. Share new learning with teacher/ class

1. Ask to move
2. Ignore friend

1. Talk to teacher
2. Different approach
3. Include personal questions
4. Ask for book
5. Involved in process/ Child as teacher

Already know information

Seating with friends

Boredom (not involved, creative individual)

Distractions

Repetition

Do not understand

1. Ask for something else to do
2. Listen again to check nothing missed
3. Make up personal challenging questions
4. Ask for quicker move to personal work if initial acquisition sound

1. Ask teacher
2. Ask a friend
3. Look back over what done
4. Move on
5. Use previous knowledge to have a go

I learn best when it is quiet

This statement is included to further explore the statement about distractions. Many mentees tell me that they need quiet to do their best learning. However, on discussion it becomes clear that most do not mean total quiet but rather with quiet music in the background. As one mentee told me, 'if it is too quiet than my mind gets locked in. I need other stimuli to keep awake.' This seems to be particularly true of the younger pupils. It is really helpful for them to realise the conditions necessary for optimal success and to consider how this may differ from task to task. Should music have words? Do certain types of music aid creative thought?

It is also essential to discuss the value of silence and the prolonged silence of exams. Experience of this is vital. Many mentees find this hard but by gradually increasing the time they spend in silent study they learn to appreciate rather than fear this space.

Link teachers have been very interested to hear the thoughts of pupils on the conditions surrounding study and to have the opportunity to use some of the ideas suggested.

Learning at school is interesting

It is extremely rare to find a pupil who scores their interest as low. When they do it seems to be linked to self-esteem. In addition, in year 12, interest almost always achieves a high score as pupils are studying subjects of their choice. In either of these instances further investigation is essential. (See Hannah's story – I feel good about myself). Pupils who score a 3 often tell me this is because learning is usually interesting but they see it as boring or uninteresting when it is new and they do not understand it or it is hard to grasp. This inextricably links to their motivation. It is also useful to consider the section on – I am inspired by the learning at school.

Case study 47

Lewis (year 12) forgot to come to the first session, so it was the end of term 1 before I got to meet him. He was not well. He gave himself a low score for self-esteem, his ability to manage stress and his interest in learning at school. He also awarded himself a five for perfectionism. He told me about his new job which took up much of his time and where he felt a valued member of the team. When he felt valued he pushed himself to succeed. Our conversation took the whole session. He needed to talk.

When we next met I started to explore with him barriers to feeling valued and how to build positivity by finding his interests. He was doing highly academic subjects but really enjoyed the creativity and freedom of some of the performing arts. As he did not feel able to join in school performances I enquired about external groups. He did not know of any. I suggested he try and find out and offered to do the same.

He told me that he thought everyone else understood quicker than him. He felt guilty. He also found it hard to speak to certain teachers. As he had two for most subjects, I suggested that he approach the one he found easiest to talk to.

By the next session I had asked my school link for local choirs, the details of which I was able to share with my mentee. Co-incidentally, one of his teachers was involved in one of them. So, I suggested he talk to him both about this opportunity and use the same conversation to broach his concerns over his work. This he agreed to do. He too had started to make enquiries although he had not yet found anything of interest.

Lewis came to our next session smiling. He had now spoken to his teacher and, as a result, had started to understand his learning more in that subject. In the event he had not mentioned the choir as a friend had told him about a local drama group which he had joined. It was highly exhilarating and great to be part of a team.

By the end of the year Lewis was making steady progress with his learning. He had discovered that drama fulfilled a vital need in him: to create. He had made some new high achieving friends with whom he had been able to talk at length. He decided to leave school and start college where he could study a mix of academic and creative subjects. He would finish his academic A2s and pick up drama. It was wonderful to see him so enthusiastic and engaged.

What would you like to learn about?

The purpose of the question at the end of the four sections is to break up the rating exercise and give the pupil time to reflect and share. The insights gained have proved extremely enlightening.

'If money or opportunity was no object what would you like to learn? It could be a new skill like belly dancing, a new language, an instrument or it could be a new subject or an extension of an old one.'

This question often catches the mentee unawares. For many it is the first time they have been asked a question like this. In life they have generally been presented with a list of options and not been given free rein to consider what really interests them. Many are keen to take up an instrument, as they have not had the opportunity before or to learn a language not offered at school. This applies just as much to those who have opted for languages at GCSE as those who have not. This provides a fascinating way to improve motivation; there is learning beyond the curriculum. (See Lucy's story in the section on stress). It also underlines the fact that the pupil needs to take responsibility for their future, to start to investigate the possibilities and opportunities; a pro-active approach is required.

Case study 48

Without hesitation Amy (year 13) replied 'architecture'. I was extremely surprised. She had just submitted her UCAS application for economics and had not studied any creative subjects at A level. Surprise quickly turned to interest and I asked her to explain. It transpired that she had always enjoyed art but as the GCSE results in art at her previous school were not good she had felt unable to pursue it. On coming to college she had considered art again but was deterred by the fact that she had not taken it at GCSE. She had regularly wandered along the art corridors and gazed at the art on display. She travelled extensively with her family and was fascinated by the different styles of architecture she saw in each country. Her aim in life was to leave a lasting legacy. She wondered if this would be possible with economics. She had told her parents (who were both in Finance) about her dream, once she had submitted her application. They were understandably shocked.

My first response was to encourage her to continue with her application whilst at the same time giving serious thought to this alternative. I advised her strongly not to pursue a course of study just because she was in the system. It may require a change of A levels, although she was already studying maths which was helpful, and a new application at a later date but in the long run this would only account for a very small amount of her life so she needed to give a lot of time to thinking through her real desires. It was essential to talk things through with her parents now they had got over the initial shock. I also suggested she start a sketch book of design aspects that interested her.

We spent several sessions coming back to this topic whilst ensuring that we focussed on her learning in general so that her A levels did not suffer. How was she to decide what to do? Initially she told me that if she did well in her economics A level then she would follow the path she had applied for. I recommended a more pro-active approach. We ordered a few prospectuses from universities offering architecture and I talked to several admissions tutors at the UCAS Design Your Future event. One university had a placement opportunity where the student spent time in an Asian environment on an architecture project which would appeal to Amy's love of foreign cultures. At the same time Amy started to go to post application days and to hear about the opportunities on offer in economics, including a period of foreign study. I challenged her – could she see herself working as an economist in 3 years' time?

I struggled to know how to help her make up her mind. Finally I decided to contact a local admissions tutor and talk through with her the characteristics of a successful applicant. What lead applicants to decide architecture was for them? She would certainly need to take an art course at some level. She was most welcome to come in and discuss her thoughts. I shared this information with Amy. She went away to think things through.

Finally she decided that economics was for her. She did not wish to take art and had found herself buying the Economist and excitedly looked forward to discussing the contents with her friends and family. We celebrated her decision. Amy told me how much she had valued the opportunity to experience an extended period of decision-making. She felt her decision-making skills had developed significantly. She was now looking forward with enthusiasm to the start of her university studies.

Case study 49

In response to this question Lauren (year 10) told me that she loved classical art and renaissance portraits. She studied extremely hard but I felt her enjoyment was limited by concentration on the curriculum content. Before our next session I picked up a selection of brochures advertising art galleries in the wider area from the stand in our local supermarket. She was very interested. We spent a while looking through them and thinking of how they could supplement her studies and also allow her to see a greater range of artists and their art. By the next session she had visited one of the galleries, completed some sketches and bought some postcards all of which enhanced her studies. She had now started an on-line search to work out where she should go next, perhaps further afield.

Lauren also enjoyed languages and was good at them. She holidayed regularly in France and was fascinated by the culture and the way language works. I brought along the list of characteristics of a G and T language student from the G and T e-bulletin produced by Optimus Education. We worked through the twelve points and highlighted those she could develop. This would entail using material beyond her current level. Lauren was particularly interested in the idea of recognising familiar language in unfamiliar contexts. She thought it would be good to do this by watching some French films. I offered to ask one of my older mentees who I knew held film nights for her friends, for some recommendations. As both mentees were in the same school, the older mentee allowed Lauren to borrow a few of them. Lauren's appreciation of language and French culture grew.

Resourcefulness

Gifted pupils can be highly resourceful, however many of those I mentor display a worrying level of passivity which can lead them to underachieve. Mentoring sessions seek to build their levels of pro-active, independent learning and to enable them to realise that this is both acceptable and highly beneficial. So often their insights and responses could be immensely useful to other pupils and their teachers if only they decided to share them.

I am good at time management

Time management is an art that has to be learnt just as much by gifted pupils as by others. Many of the pupils I mentor are very busy both at school and at home, so need to balance many demands. Ironically it is often those who are busiest who are best at managing their time. Some however, need a sounding board to help them sort out competing commitments (Bethany case study 26) and others need to analyse the issue and set themselves personal targets to resolve it (Jordan case study 23). For some mentees their issues are just in one area such as deadlines, homework or long-term projects and their stories feature in the relevant sections. Many though struggle with time management *per se*. They benefit from time spent thinking through the issue, what they would like to achieve, what is realistic, what they personally need to do and anything the school could do to help. Many have never undertaken such an exercise before; however many have some wonderful solutions. This is particularly important as they start sixth form as work is more demanding and often extended, independent study is essential.

Case study 50

Eleanor (year 13) told me she was generally good at time management but she did not always find enough time for music practice, which she needed to do as she had two exams coming up later in the year. We talked through her commitments, including her Saturday job and her workload. I was pleased to hear that she also found time to meet with friends. Eleanor definitely did not want to do a schedule as she thought this was very boring. I thought her reaction was interesting. This was just the same response as pupils who did not do a revision schedule, because they had done one once and it had not worked and they assumed this was the only model available. I suggested a changing timetable linked to actual tasks for the week. Eleanor was intrigued. I asked her to go away and make one for that week and then the next and come and tell me how it worked.

Eleanor reported back that the rolling timetable had been useful. She had maintained the same one for two weeks as her commitments and work load had been the same but now she had changed it as several subjects had set revision which she needed to tackle in a different way across time. She had found time to fit in her music practice by practicing each instrument at length on alternate days. She realised that in the past she had always done what she liked or was best at first and left the harder, less pleasant tasks until later. Now she had decided to ensure she did a mix of easier and more difficult tasks each day and had started to find that some of her less pleasant tasks were in fact not so bad now that she was tackling them with time to spare. Eleanor's time management was now the result of conscious planning.

Case study 51
Olivia (year 13) had achieved very highly at GCSE but her AS level results were not as good as she had hoped. She told me that she had decided therefore not to set targets as she was scared of failure. It soon became clear that she had also applied the same philosophy to time management. Olivia seemed to be in a constant muddle and to be running to keep up with herself. She desperately wanted to learn to drive so often accepted extra shifts at work in order to finance this. I assured her that success was possible. We talked through the reasons for her difficulties and what an organised life would look like for her. We decided to start with a target she could quickly achieve; sort out and file her notes on a daily basis. This she saw as the strength of our sessions. I would challenge her, we would agree a smart target and she would achieve it.

I questioned the hours she was working. Olivia told me that it was just over the Christmas period and whilst she was learning to drive. She would definitely cut down during the January mocks. We put together a list of all the tasks she needed to complete to revise well in each of her subjects. I sent her home to work out a time 'guesstimate' for each task and then, working backwards from the date of each exam, to create a schedule, taking into account her other commitments and ensuring she did not overload herself. She would then be in an informed position to negotiate working hours.

By the next time I saw Olivia, she had completed her exams. They had gone well and her working hours had decreased significantly. She had not made a full schedule as suggested but it was clear the thought process had helped her put her life in perspective. I continued to mentor Olivia every three months until the summer exams. She never did make a complete schedule but she halved her working hours and started to talk to her teachers which enabled her to gain a clearer picture of the steps she needed to take to achieve the highest grades. She was accepted at the university of her choice.

Case study 52
Courtney (year 10) was highly stressed. She did not enjoy school and her self-esteem was extremely low. I asked her what she would like to tackle first. Organisation, she decided. I asked her to tell me about a time when she was organised. She could not think of one. So we moved on to consider the issues as she saw them. There were several. The first thing she mentioned was that she carried all her books around with her to stop her forgetting them. I explained that although this solved the problem it did not address it. Her first target was to pack her bag each night using her timetable as a prompt. This would allow her to take control of the issue rather than it controlling her.

Her next issue was that homework was often submitted late. We talked through each subject, looking at the sort of homework set and how long it took. As there was no school homework timetable, I asked her to come up with a solution. Initially she told me she did not know but after a number of additional questions she decided that it would be a good idea to look at her planner on a Friday night and then plan her homework schedule for the coming week.

At our next meeting she told me that the bag packing was going well. Her bag was now much lighter! Her mum had helped too by buying her a posh planner. Her homework was generally getting done on time now. Revision for tests was the next focus. She rarely remembered test dates until just before they happened which left her with too little revision time. We talked through how much time she thought she needed and planned the revision in blocks into her schedule. This helped relieve her stress but it also highlighted how uninspired she was by much of her learning and homework. I suggested we share this with the school and she agreed, asking me to speak to my link teacher.

Case study 53
Luke (year 10) thought it would help him to spread his work out across time. He would like this skill. If he did so he was sure his marks would improve as he would have longer to consider his homework task more deeply and to ask for help if necessary. He had already tried doing his French writing over an extended period and had got an A. He decided to apply this to his French speaking and to do his maths homework when set so that he had time to ask questions if necessary. Luke tackled his homework the very next day on 'My Maths' and, finding that he got a few wrong, he had time to go back, use complex formula and eventually

get them right. He would definitely repeat this idea again. He also reported that he now felt more confident with his speaking.

After several more mentoring sessions, I was delighted when Luke arrived one day, in the midst of the exam period, and told me that he had decided he needed to change his routine to allow him to give of his best. He now showered in the morning which helped him to wake up as he was not a good morning person. He ate a good breakfast of porridge, fruit juice and tea then walked to school without his usual last minute dash. In the evening he was not rushing around but sitting down quietly with his revision guide. He was in bed by 10.30pm. This was only during the exam period though! Luke had certainly learnt the benefit of good time management.

Case study 54
Holly (year 11) was concerned about the period of independent study in the run up to the exams. She was highly conscientious but so used to being organised by school that she was concerned she would not get the most out of this time. We talked through each subject, as with Olivia in case study 51. She had some very creative and individual ideas about how to revise different subjects. I stressed that the revision period was not a life sentence and it was quite permissible, indeed necessary, for her to get outside for some breaks. This could include meeting with friends with whom she decided to cycle whilst testing each other on various topics. Holly produced a very good schedule which achieved her revision objectives whilst not overloading her. She was well prepared for her transition to independent study at college in year 12.

Case study 55
Megan (year 13) found essay writing stressful, it was so difficult to fit in all the study time she needed. I asked her if there was anyone else in her class who seemed to manage this well. She told me that Molly, her best friend, who was also doing English and history, was amazing. She was a motivated, A* student who knew she had to work to a good standard whereas others did this at half-mast. She was very good at finding time to do her work. The previous week Molly had written much of her essay in the car on the way back from her Grandma's. 'I could never do that!' Megan told me. I knew Molly as she was also one of my mentees. She had already told me about this episode. It was the only way she could complete her work on time whilst also fitting in a family trip. I explained to Megan that this was called making the most of 'down time'. I wondered if she had any. It transpired that every two weeks she travelled on two trains to visit her boyfriend. Could she make the most of this time I wondered?

It seemed that the second train was standing room only but the first one was always fairly quiet. Megan decided to have a go.

Next time I saw Megan she was enthusiastic about how well it had gone. She had decided to travel in the quiet carriage so that she was not disturbed by other people's mobile phone conversations. The silence had enabled her to get deep into her text. She got through a great deal in the time! By doing this on the outward and return journey she gained two hours. She was able to have a more relaxed weekend and then use her study time at school to write instead of trying to read and think which she found really hard at school. We considered whether she could benefit by following the example of any other expert.

I always meet deadlines

The vast majority of those I have mentored manage to meet deadlines even if this means they work late the night before or submit sub-standard work. There are a few however who, with some simple suggestions, improve their deadline management significantly and also their performance.

Case study 56

Alexander (year 12) was a very quiet pupil who rarely made eye contact. He said little and I often wondered if he was fully engaging with the process. However, each time we set a target he completed it just as set. His organisation was not good. He sometimes did not do his homework or gave it in late. Why was this I wondered? The answer was simple. He did not write down what was set and so either could not remember what he was supposed to do or forgot altogether. Had this always been a problem I enquired? In fact, although it had started to be an issue late into GCSEs, it was this year that it had become a major problem. In the early years of secondary school homework was always set for the next couple of days. In addition everyone had the same so they helped each other remember. Now the time spans were much longer and at college there was much greater subject diversity among students. I challenged him to take control of the situation. What could he do to solve this problem? He could obtain a planner to write it down and stop relying on deadline prompts from others.

At our next session Alexander explained that he had not bought a planner but he had started to use the appointments section on his phone to record homework or tests. Now much more homework was being done and on time. What would it take to catch up completely I asked? He thought hard and told me the backlog involved corrections he had to make following initial marking of homework. When pushed to estimate how long it would take to complete, he calculated about an hour. This was his next target. Sensing he was on board I also set a 'radical target'. He was to do his homework when set. This raised a smile. By the next session he was completely up to date.

Case study 57

Harry (year 10) had a problem with homework deadlines. Upon investigation I discovered that he had been given three essays by three different subject teachers all for completion in the same time frame. He had found it impossible to produce them all to a high standard in the given time, so one was submitted late. I asked him what else he could have done. Write shorter, less detailed essays he suggested. Had he not considered renegotiating the deadline? He had not. I explained that in a secondary school different faculties do not always talk to each other and so one teacher is not necessarily aware of the homework set by another. Each teacher however wants their pupils to do well and would therefore be open to reconsideration if they knew the deadline was problematic. This realisation gave him the knowledge to be an active partner in his learning.

I manage long-term projects well

The art of managing long-term projects whether with regard to lengthy pieces of work or projects or alternatively a long-term focus on achieving the higher grades requires great staying power or 'grit' and high levels of resourcefulness and reflectiveness. Girls with low-esteem and quite a number of boys seem to struggle the most as do younger pupils. For many the hardest part is actually starting. As one mentee told me 'I really enjoy the challenge once I am into my work, it's getting started at all that's the real problem'. For others knowing how to start is the hardest part. Many benefit from instruction in how to break the task down into manageable chunks to stop it becoming too arduous, with 'rewards' to mark each milestone achieved such as time to watch a favourite TV programme. The ability to calculate correctly the time needed to complete a task is one that requires much practice, allowing pupils to achieve not only final but interim deadlines as well. It is a highly valuable life skill.

Relevant case studies also appear in the sections on weaknesses and perfectionism.

Case study 58
Joseph (year 13) identified long-term planning as an issue. This would be very useful with his maths coursework. We talked about how to break the task down into stages and guesstimate the time needed for each part. Joseph undertook to try this at home. I asked him to monitor how it went and at the end to reflect on any possible improvements he could make.

Joseph tackled this objective the same day. He made a timetable and stuck to it. He intentionally gave himself quite generous time slots. In fact as he did not need all the time allowed he finished early and so had time for a second draft which he had now handed in. His relief and contentment were self-evident. On reflection he realised that this methodology had also helped him to manage distractions more effectively. He knew he needed to complete each stage of his work in a set time frame and so left his former distractions as a reward for later when he could enjoy them properly.

Case study 59
Our daughter Charlotte took English for A level. She was aiming for and was expected to achieve an A at AS level. From October to April she had a maternity cover teacher. When her own teacher returned she assessed the class to see how they were doing. Many were not reaching their targets. Charlotte was working at a B. She was horrified. Charlotte was determined to rectify this. In consultation

with her teacher she mapped out what she needed to do to achieve her goal. There was not long. It would be necessary to complete an essay every week to practice writing at the correct level. She began. After each essay was marked she devoured the comments and then applied lessons learnt to the next one. In June she achieved her A and the following year got a distinction in her additional English paper.

I have used this story several times with mentees to show them how a long-term goal can be reached and to underline the focus, organisation and determination necessary.

I manage my homework well

Very few mentees regard homework as a major issue. There are moments when, with all their activities and commitments, it is not done as well as they would have liked or is late and occasionally is not done at all. Generally though, it is an accepted part of their weekly routine. Some however, struggle with the content of the homework set or their organisation and technique. Allowing time for discussion frees them to come up with creative solutions.

The most able sixth formers sometimes question exercises set. One year 13 told me that he loved the challenge of long-term projects but he saw some of the shorter pieces as unnecessary or unhelpful. He knew he could acquire the required knowledge using another quicker method. It had not occurred to him to quietly share his insights with his teacher for the benefit of all. Several mentees, through discussion, have virtually had a 'eureka' moment as they have come up with effective solutions. One realised she could use bullet points when annotating her art thus allowing her to cover a large amount of information in a short space of time, another that a good way to remember all her homework was to produce a list by her bed which she highlighted as pieces were completed. Others have understood that they can improve performance by breaking up their tasks and accomplishing them over time. New technology has also been extremely helpful. One sixth former, whilst exploring all the functions of her new phone, discovered that she could use it to plan her work schedule. She obtained great satisfaction by ticking off the tasks each day.

For a small number, the homework struggle highlights other issues such as lack of confidence, an ineffective family model, undiagnosed special needs or 'hidden' external factors. An example of this can be found under other factors. Homework issues are also covered under stress and time management.

Case study 60

Hannah (year 10) had a marked lack of confidence in maths, which affected the way she did her homework. I asked her to talk me through this. Each time she started well and progressed until she came to a question she could not do. She then doubted herself, rang a friend and if they could not help her, missed it out. Occasionally she also looked at useful web-sites. She did not have the confidence to talk to her teacher. She agreed I could speak to my link teacher.

At our next session she reported that her maths teacher had spent some time with her and reassured her that she was always happy to help. Hannah started to make progress.

Case study 61

Tom (year 10) found homework stressful. He always left it to the night before. He wanted to change but was not sure how to. As there was no school homework timetable he never knew what to expect. We discussed what he would find must helpful. He agreed to go away and design a flexible schedule that he could fit around whatever homework he had with the emphasis on completing work as soon as possible after it was set.

When he came to see me two weeks later, he told me that he had decided to set himself blocks of time for homework or relaxation. This was working well. It meant he was more focussed and with the reward of football, Xbox or TV to look forward to his mood lifted, which impacted positively on the work he produced.

Case study 62

Jade (year 13) was highly creative. She had so many projects on the go and ideas for activities that she struggled to remember everything or to fit it all in. I told her about an exercise I had tried with my own daughter who was also very creative and involved in many school and extra- curricular activities. We had written down all the different tasks and then divided them into three piles; must do now, must do but deadline is later, may do in the future. This then allowed her to prioritise. Each day she tackled the urgent and tried to also start some of the tasks in the second pile. Future possibilities were considered over time, some took place and others did not.

This system appealed to Jade. She could not wait to get home and try it out. At our next session she said it had greatly helped her decide her priorities for the day and the week. She had added an element of her own. As visual stimuli were particularly important to her she had bought herself a whiteboard. She then listed her current daily and weekly tasks and rubbed them off as they were completed. This she found extremely satisfying and also great fun.

I ask big questions

Gifted young people have a huge capacity for deep, innovative, creative thought. Early on in my mentoring experience, in answer to the question 'Tell me about a good question you have asked', a six year old told me that he had asked his teacher 'What are germs made of?' His Dad had then helped him to explore the answer. My son Isaac, before he started school, regularly looked at the design of things and played with their moving parts, asking himself how he could apply this mechanism in a different context. His junk-modelling creations attempted to formulate a prototype from his ideas. So we had the coffee-making machine that also washed up the cups using the principle of the three button approach found in the hand-washing area of public toilets. Sadly this heightened state of curiosity is often lost during their specification-led education, where there is seemingly little time to ask questions, to pause for thought. Many of my year 10 and 11s state that they do not ask many, or even any, big questions. Reasons given are a lack of time in or between lessons, homework overload and anxieties about deadlines. Worryingly some even wonder why this would be necessary when they understand the curriculum. Why would they need or want to go further? This situation usually improves when they embark on sixth form study and certainly big questions are prevalent amongst those achieving highly at this level. The less confident and less well-organised student often sadly neglects the value of thinking time. In all cases boys seem to be more likely to pose the most searching questions.

Quite a number of mentees are unsure of the term 'big question'. We talk about questions, often with no single right or wrong answer, which move our learning on or take it to another plane, engendering critical thinking and which allow us to play with and manipulate ideas. We often try out a series of fun debates considering questions such as 'Would you rather be stuck in a lift with a wasp or a fly?' or 'What if there were no colours?' This then leads on to the consideration of areas they would like to explore or questions they could ask linked to their personal passions (see passions diagram on p. 131). We also look at the idea of deductions or inferences using a certain amount of knowledge to consider possible issues and outcomes. I find the example of my personal considerations about the 'stumbling' of certain gifted pupils illustrates this well. Pupils also benefit greatly from G and T in-school or inter-school questioning days, allowing them to consider how to ask a good question and to reflect on the benefits for their learning.

Some of my most highly-reflective mentees self-impose a ceiling to their questioning. In class they question how something could be proved and then often internally expand their thinking but do not verbalise it as they feel this level of insight is not required in the class setting. Others share their big questions and find these are not welcomed. One insightful pupil told me she thought it is assumed by teachers such questions would confuse other pupils and compromise the time needed to get through the syllabus.

My mentees and I have considered a range of personalised ways forward. In addition, some have spoken to teachers out of class or joined or started a club or study-group either in school or externally, where they can share and explore with other like-minded young people a subject area of their choice. Some have started a debating society. Others have joined on-line forums run by a range of organisations. The IGGY forum, a global online network for gifted students has proved particularly rewarding. Sometimes it has been possible to pair mentees with an 'ementor', a university student studying a subject in which they are interested and about which they can converse.

It is helpful to refer to the section on confidence as a lack of confidence is a major factor in limiting the asking of both small and big questions.

Case study 63
Sarah (year 10) had spent several mentoring sessions with me working on building her confidence. In history she wanted to be more confident when answering questions. The teacher made her very anxious as he operated a no hands up policy when asking questions and Sarah hated being put on the spot. It was important to her to be right. We started thinking about ways to address this and to be better prepared. I explained that it was quite acceptable to pause before answering, to allow time for thought. In fact this was the move of a reflective person. She was greatly relieved. This had never occurred to her before. I assured her that it was also fine to be wrong but she was not at all convinced. Sarah always prepared well in advance, she hated to be rushed. I suggested therefore that another solution would be to build in thinking time for each topic at home so that she felt better able to answer questions posed. Together we put together a list of possible sources of information. As a target I asked her to think about her current topic and to consider what sort of question might be posed and what she would like to know or consider. This was a new experience for Sarah. She was used to doing what she was asked and not to thinking deeply for herself.

By our next session Sarah had read ahead in her textbook and watched a relevant programme on television. She recounted to me what she had learnt and the questions she had generated about warfare. I posed a few more. We agreed to watch the same series the following week and to share our findings. Little by little Sarah started to allow herself to think deeply. Her enjoyment of history grew as did her confidence. She was less worried about answering class questions and the scope and depth of her questioning expanded.

Case study 64

Olivia (year 13) was very anxious about her grades. I suggested we formulate a plan to take away her anxiety. We looked particularly at how to take her learning forward in philosophy, her favourite subject, but ironically the one on which she spent the least amount of time due to the workload in the other subjects. The anxiety would be decreased if she felt more in control. We considered how to deepen her knowledge. She had excellent questioning skills that she had acquired from this subject discipline. Where should she focus her time and thoughts? Her major interest was the philosophy of religion. So we set a target that she would spend ten minutes a day reading, which would rekindle her interest without overburdening her. She would also listen to podcasts, which she could do whilst walking to college.

The next time I saw Olivia she told me about the material she had covered and her thought processes. The ten minute target had grown to twenty, as once she had started reading she found it hard to stop. She had found that the reading and listening had triggered a number of questions in her mind some of which she had then been able to share in class discussion and others she had included in her next piece of work. Olivia's interest and enthusiasm grew. Her focus shifted from exams to the enjoyment of her learning. She was now making greater progress and spending more in depth time on philosophy but in such a way that there was still enough time for everything else.

Case study 65

Rebecca (year 10) was very shy and anxious. You can read her story in the section on confidence. We worked on enabling her to speak to teachers and also to ask questions in class. Following an inter-school questioning day I asked her how she thought she could use questioning to deepen her learning. She was terrified of class or large group discussion but said that although she did not share her ideas she often wondered quietly. In fact she had asked a friend round that evening to talk through the science topic that she was struggling to understand. As a target I suggested that once the topic became clearer they formulate a 'big' question and discuss how to explore it.

At our next session Rebecca quietly told me that she and her friend had cracked the science and then spent some time thinking about where they could go next. To her amazement, the teacher addressed their 'big' question in the next lesson. Rebecca's understanding and confidence grew. Over time she acquired a number of learning partners for different subjects.

Case study 66

Danielle (year 13) did not think she was good at asking 'big' questions. We considered what a 'big' question might look like and then set about applying this to each of her A level subjects; biology, chemistry and French. In biology she wondered why there was a specific change in one strand of DNA and not in another. She agreed to do some personal research and then if necessary speak to her teacher. In chemistry each student was already required to do an individual research project. She was investigating the level of vitamin C content in cooked and uncooked vegetables. This was posing multiple questions. In French she wanted to consider how the different aspects of Truffaut's character are shown in his films. She and her friends had set up a series of film nights in order to view a large number of his films. I suggested to her that in fact she was already well underway in developing her questioning skills. She now needed to do this more pro-actively and more often.

Soon after this Danielle asked me for an extra session to practice for a group interview as part of her university application process. We worked on how to think outside the box and express one's opinions whilst also including others and acknowledging their contributions. I was delighted when she returned and recounted to me how the interview went. She had been asked: What is the most important discovery of the modern age? Having recently been on a residential course about neurology she chose to nominate the brain and to talk about the many recent discoveries about its capacity. I was delighted that she had taken our consideration of 'big' questions on board and applied it to her wider learning, making links with previous learning and presenting it in a new context. It was evident to me that she had understood the concept of playing with her learning and manipulating it. She was offered a place.

Case study 67

Shannon (year 10) had begun to realise her inner questions were of great value and that her unique perspective was one to celebrate and share rather than to nervously hide (see the section on confidence). She very definitely already had the ability to ask 'big' deep questions. What she needed now was the encouragement to take this further. We compiled a 'passions' diagram (see Three useful diagrams on pp. 127–31). She chose to research a combination of two of her interests, those of animals and the environment. Several weeks later she brought along her findings to date. I was extremely impressed to see the breadth of her sources. We talked through what she had discovered about the effects of the environment on animal habitat. She was fascinated. This was just the start. Her research was the catalyst to much deeper exploration. My initial suggestion had stressed the importance of ensuring this additional task did not overload her schedule. It was no longer a task, it had become a part of her.

Case study 68

Oliver (year 13) had not achieved high grades in his AS exams. We set about exploring how to help him as a learner. It quickly became apparent that he had huge insights but his achievement was hampered as the syllabus was not posing questions in which he was really interested. It was too limited and rigid. He read widely, particularly in engineering, and then applied lessons learnt at his work in an outward bound shop where he tinkered with repairs on bikes. Customers frequently sought his advice and through their questioning he had developed a deep understanding of the working of the products. He also learnt by using the products in his free time. He proudly told me that his knowledge of rope force had greatly helped him in physics. Oliver was undoubtedly a self-motivated learner but he risked being 'failed' by the school system. He needed a more practical education. He had considered the possibility of an apprenticeship and had looked at a few. I sent him the link to apprenticeships. He started to apply. Ultimately he beat hundreds of others to gain an apprenticeship in electronic engineering at a highly regarded company. He now had an outlet for his 'big' questions.

I sometimes do not understand my learning

Until very recently this statement read I 'often' do not understand my learning. Mentees stated that this was not the case. However, through exploring other responses such as their confidence rating (see the section on confidence), it was evident that a lack of understanding at times caused mentees to stumble, maybe to ignore the current learning focus and sometimes even to give up. This only came to light however when delving deeper into initial responses. This statement has therefore been changed to enable this issue to be highlighted more easily. It may still not reveal the true picture as mentees are often loathe to openly admit to a lack of understanding. The belief that this 'weakness' is unacceptable in a gifted pupil remains strong. However the inclusion of the statement will emphasise this possibility for mentees.

One area where mentees do admit to a lack of understanding is in the area of exam questions where on occasion they 'mess up' a paper by overcomplicating their understanding and therefore ignore the simple, straightforward and correct answer.

Case study 69

Adam (year 13) was an excellent mathematician. He loved to play with theories and manipulate data. He had been offered a conditional place at a leading university to read economics and needed an A to achieve this. In the summer he sat two exam papers. After the first paper he went home distraught. His mother telephoned the school and asked that someone speak to him urgently. Later that day he came back in. He had worked hard for the exam and knew the material well. However, when he had read the exam paper he had decided that the questions could not possibly be as simple as they seemed. So, he had thought very hard and answered them at a level he thought would be what was expected at A level. After the exam, the comments of other pupils made him realise this had been unnecessary. He had over-complicated the paper. His maths teachers spent a long time talking him through each response and strategizing with him. As I was in school that day I then spent some time helping to re-build his self-esteem. This enabled him to tackle the remaining exams in a positive manner. On results day, he lost quite a lot of marks on the first paper but, as his other maths marks were very high, he still achieved his A.

Learning is often challenging

Challenge is essential. Pupils need to learn how to struggle and maybe even 'fail' safely to build their resilience and also to grow their resourcefulness.

Mentee responses to this statement are very mixed. Challenge is at its highest in the transition from year 11 to year 12. Pupils often comment on how hard they find the adjustment. They struggle with independent study, longer time spans for work, the pace and level of learning.

In year 10 and 11 many pupils have told me that they rarely experience challenge. Their learning is continually directed and supported by their teachers. In one school the first time real challenge occurred was when pupils sat a mock science exam under a new format and with a revised mark scheme, which meant that most gained a very low grade. They were horrified but I explained how valuable this experience was. They had temporarily floundered but still had time to rectify this and to consider personal strategies for dealing with demanding situations in the future. In effect it ultimately brought out the best in them as they worked really hard to understand what was required of them and to address the situation. Some sadly find that expectations are regularly low and I work with them on finding ways to take their learning forward using ideas from the 'big' questions section. To counter this many decide to choose an A level subject that they know will challenge them. It is their way of building in challenge for themselves. Challenge however is present for some and this often comes when learning is new and hard or they do not understand it, or where they are asked to work independently on certain topics. Being put on the spot in class questioning is also mentioned as is learning that cannot be mastered quickly or that requires more than one explanation by the teacher.

In year 13 the existence of challenge seems dependant on subject chosen, teaching methods, specification content or individual teachers. Some pupils are highly challenged as with some of my chemistry mentees who had to design and execute an experiment from start to finish (see the section on expectations). Others never experience real challenge and benefit from encouragement to seek it or briefing about how challenge will feel at university in order to counter the detrimental effect this could have on their resilience when they perceive that others are cleverer than them and learning is hard. The Extended Project Qualification is often very useful in helping them challenge themselves.

How to address challenge is featured throughout this book and particularly in the sections on confidence, self-esteem, understanding learning, risk-taking and expectations of others.

Case study 70

Our son Noel (year 11) greatly enjoyed French. Modern foreign languages were not compulsory at his school so the classes were small and mixed ability. He found therefore that he was easily able to assimilate the material covered. Keen to maintain his interest I suggested that he ask the teacher to recommend a French magazine he could read to supplement his learning. Noel was delighted to be leant a magazine on winter sports, something that he had very much enjoyed on the one occasion he had been snowboarding. He found the text demanding but not impossible and enjoyed puzzling over certain grammatical structures and selecting a few good phrases to use in his written work. They also came in very handy in his oral.

Case study 71

Abigail (year 13) was a highly gifted pupil. She studied hard and was also very popular and enjoyed socialising with friends. In our final session, before Abigail left for study leave, as we thought back over all she had learnt and considered how prepared she was for university study, I asked her if she had ever really found her learning challenging. This had never been the case. I talked her through university study and explained that she would most certainly experience challenge here. This, coupled with two expected low points in November and February when she would have a lot of work and the weather would undoubtedly be dismal, could cause her to question her ability and to struggle. I reassured her that this was quite normal and we talked about how to resolve this situation and who she could talk to if necessary. She would not be alone, most other people would experience struggle too.

I heard from Abigail towards the end of her first year. There had indeed been much more challenge at university. There was a lot more to remember so revision had to start much earlier for each exam and an assumption that students consolidated their knowledge outside of lectures. The content was much harder and some topics she found difficult to get her head around. However, our discussion and the warnings given by tutors and lecturers that it would not be possible just to 'breeze' through the year had definitely helped. She had been well prepared for the change.

Learning is well paced

This statement has proved useful as have others in helping mentees to think through some of the underlying issues that combine to undermine their performance as a learner. None of them have chosen to focus on this statement itself but it is certainly a factor in explaining frustration or lack of understanding.

In general my mentees have been happy with the pace of learning. However, occasionally those in mixed ability classes, particularly at GCSE, have told me of highly frustrating lessons when material has been explained very slowly and revisited several times to meet the needs of lower ability pupils and in the meantime some of the higher ability pupils have become disruptive. We consider what they could do to address this and they often have very insightful solutions, although sometimes they feel powerless to act. In this instance, with their permission, I refer the matter to my link teacher.

I have also encountered a number of mentees who are unnerved or frustrated by the speed of learning. Gifted pupils do not necessarily process their learning at speed and several have mentioned their need for adequate thinking time either in questioning sessions or before applying what they have been taught (see 'the style of teaching and learning' and 'other factors').

I get frustrated by the learning at school

Frustration can be a major issue for gifted pupils. Across the years I have had many conversations with young people and their parents about frustration caused by the pace of learning (too fast to allow deep thought or to address insights beyond the syllabus or alternatively too slow), the number of examples of a similar level pupils are required to complete to show they have grasped a concept and the time sometimes spent recapping or reworking explanations until everyone has understood. When frustration is not addressed this can quickly lead to desperation resulting in loss of interest, disruptiveness or despondency and ultimately even depression. As a parent I have first-hand experience of this downward spiral.

I am delighted however, that in recent mentoring of years 10-13 the response to this question was significant in that a huge percentage gave it a low rating, including the largest number of zero ratings across the whole questionnaire. A small percentage of mentees gave a medium score as although they were not generally frustrated there were specific times when they were and almost no-one felt greatly frustrated. When frustration occurred it was caused either by certain school systems such as enforced, prescribed in-school revision or by the methods or contradictory requirements of certain teachers. In addition it was mentioned that teachers spent much time with the less able and relatively little with them. At times there was also frustration at the choice or content of study (see – 'What subject do you most enjoy?'). Some pupils have told me that they would love to be able to choose what to study in their subject area and to explore it in depth for themselves.

Case study 72

Jake (year 13) was very frustrated by the homework tasks set in biology. The pupils were issued with a topic pack, which was a good idea, but the requirement to work through a number of set exercises in order to acquire the necessary knowledge greatly frustrated him as he knew he could achieve this knowledge acquisition much more quickly and effectively through personal reading. I set him the target of talking to his teacher about the issue. At the next session he told me that she had not used this technique again so he had not spoken to her. I sensed a diffidence in speaking to teachers. Jake was reading extensively around the topic and was also in the process of attending several interviews for medicine. I asked him to speak to her about both what he had learnt and his interview experience.

At our following session Jake informed me that he had spoken to his teacher about his interviews and told her about the wonderful facilities he had seen when touring around the various medical departments. He had still not shared his reading. 'So why is that?' I asked. He did not think it was very cool. In further discussion I discovered that all those with whom he had been at school up to GCSEs had left at sixteen to get a job. He was the only one in education and thinking of going to university. He was not used to talking to teachers on a level about the subject matter. I in turn explained how delighted staff were to find pupils who shared their passion for a subject and that they loved to talk about new findings and ideas. I again encouraged him to find a moment to speak to her. He did not do so. Outwardly he was a highly confidant individual but his background really limited him in certain ways.

When the results of the mocks were released, Jake discovered that he had achieved excellent grades. The teacher now realised that his methods worked for him and no longer insisted he take notes in class but let him follow the text book. She also tried to push him further by putting up some more work for him to do when he finished before the others. Sadly this was more of the same. I continued to encourage him to speak to her and also suggested that at university he would find it highly beneficial to debate and discuss with his lecturers. Jake received a number of offers to study medicine and achieved the grades to do so.

Case study 73
Alice (year 11) was fascinated by science. She read widely and thought deeply. She asked me to help her with her questioning technique as she told me that her science teacher did not seem to answer her questions. Sometimes in lessons she did not understand the answer given and so asked to have the concept explained again. She found that the teacher used the same illustration as before and so she still did not understand. Determined to increase her understanding she went home and researched the concept for herself, using high level sites and thinking through the information she found until she felt confidant with her own understanding. She wondered what to do in future to achieve better dialogue. She really wanted to share her new-found understanding as not to do so took away the fun of finding out. I told her that when I was at school I had a physics teacher who repeated her explanations and as I did not understand the explanation the first time, I did not understand the same one the second time either. Both teachers were so sure in their own minds of the clarity of their explanation that they sadly seemed unable to comprehend that others struggled. I suggested that Alice find a quiet moment to let the teacher know that she now understood the principle and to share the explanation that had worked for her.

In this way the teacher would have the opportunity to benefit from a different viewpoint and realise that pupils understood in different ways. Alice found a quiet moment and spoke to her teacher who nodded. I encouraged her to persevere and maybe to include her personal explanation in her written work as her teacher would read this when she was not distracted by the needs of the class.

I am inspired by the learning at school

It is interesting to compare the response to this statement to that given to frustration. Although most pupils are definitely not frustrated by their learning, they are not necessarily inspired. Mentees are often quite ambivalent in year 10 and 11 as some subjects enthuse them and others do not. Year 12s are often more inspired but some are initially too specification focussed to allow inspiration to take place. Year 13s are generally much more inspired but there is still a significant number who are more ambivalent or uninspired. This is often the case for those who are already far beyond the learning offered at school and see the menu on offer as highly simplistic and limiting. Low self-esteem, on-going transition difficulties or anxiety about future direction also hamper inspiration.

Many mentees choose to focus on inspiration thereby increasing motivation. As a mentor, I find this particularly rewarding. I challenge mentees to find a way to take their learning further and deeper, to explore the possibilities and to find an area, maybe outside the curriculum or a new subject available at university, which truly inspires them. Examples illustrated elsewhere in the book are Josh's story (8) and Lauren's story (9) about talking to enthusiasts, Shannon's story (67) using research inspired by her passions and also Emily's stories (6) and (37) building on aspirations and increasing confidence by asking wondering questions.

Case study 74
Liam, one of my year 11 mentees, hotly debated the idea of inspiration as he felt this was not something to be expected at school, it was too strong a word. He was an extremely high achiever and did so with relatively little effort. However he had not yet found something which truly gripped his attention and fired his enthusiasm. We talked through his subjects. He particularly enjoyed sport and was part of various school teams and an external football team. Maybe one day he would gain a sport scholarship to study in America. His club was monitoring his progress. He also enjoyed drama but had not taken this beyond lessons due to his sporting commitments. We considered areas outside the curriculum. He told me that he had decided to read a book about Genghis Khan recommended by his favourite cousin. He had greatly enjoyed it and animatedly recounted the highlights. I wondered if this had inspired him to read anything else or to explore further. It had not. He was not allowing himself to be drawn into further activity or study. For Liam the important thing was to maintain his status but he did not expect to have to put undue effort into this. I asked him to start a scrapbook of anything that interested him; books, song lyrics, sports players, famous discoveries. He struggled to do so.

We started to discuss his A level choice. It was evident that his choice was influenced by those subjects he thought he could do well in without risking too much challenge. I notified my link teacher to allow the school to monitor the situation. At the same time he achieved a B for a mock exam in which he expected an A. This gave me the opportunity to talk through the importance of hard work and to re-iterate that this was the move of a gifted learner. We researched sport scholarships for sports science courses or to open the door to other areas of study. Liam became more interested. I described the difficulties gifted young people who have not had to struggle lower down the school often face in transition to sixth form. He began to take note. Little by little I sensed that he was realising that his future progress and enjoyment of studies depended on his personal effort and motivation. As he left on study leave I reminded him about the scrapbook. The long summer holiday would provide lots of time for this. As a precursor we spent the last session looking through a number of university prospectuses to explore different subjects available, what they involved and to what they could lead. He left planning what he would read next and what films he could watch to take his interests further.

Case study 75
George (year 9) really enjoyed history but wanted to be more inspired. He was currently looking at world war two. I asked him what he would suggest. He told me that his Dad had a bookcase full of books on military history. His first target was to read the first ten pages of one and to come back and tell me about it. At the following session, as he recounted what he had read, he was amazed to discover how much he had learnt from just ten pages, which had really not taken him long to read. He agreed to share his learning with his teacher who was very interested and impressed.

He then chose to try and see relevance in his learning. His target was to ask his maths teacher how a certain topic was relevant to real life. During this conversation he mentioned what he had learnt from his reading about the bouncing bomb and this lead to a discussion about another use of maths. George was delighted. A while later I heard from another of his teachers that George had become much more engaged in his learning.

Case study 76
Luke (year 10) was particularly enjoying science. He intended to study in this field at university. I suggested he take his studies further perhaps by using *Minute Physics* on *You Tube,* which another mentee had recommended. At the next session he would present to me what he had learnt. He chose to focus on space linked to a fascinating area of study he remembered from year 8.

Luke told me clearly about the life of stars and how they formed. He would now like to know what made the whole process work. We discussed how he could find out. He decided to ask his teacher to recommend some sources. His excitement was tangible.

Case study 77

Eleanor (year 13) worked hard but showed no emotion and saw herself as average. We discussed the idea of inspiration. I asked her to talk me through what she enjoyed about each of her subjects. She was particularly interested in law, which she had applied to study at university. She loved methodically working through cases and reading about real people. It was fascinating to see how it applied to everything around and items in the news. Insanity cases, crimes involving sleep-walking interested her most. I asked how she could take this further. She explained that when she was really interested she used Google to find further information and read the *Independent*. Class discussions also helped. Her enthusiasm did not show outwardly but in her own way she was taking her learning forward. She developed this significantly once she started university.

Case study 78

Elizabeth (year 12) had achieved extremely highly at GCSE. She told me that although she was very consistent she was not top at anything. She had set her sights on dentistry so only top grades would do. Her work ethic was good but she found the transition to sixth form level studies hard. As we filled in her questionnaire it became clear that her focus was on grades. She identified a weakness as solving problems but not looking at the reasons and memorising well but not looking at the information behind the facts. She did not often ask big questions or take risks in her learning. Any independent study was to fulfil grade requirements rather than to fulfil her curiosity. Her stress levels were high.

This came to a head in the January mocks when virtually the whole class got E or U in one of the sciences. She needed to learn how to study smarter. I suggested she acquire a more detailed text book that went beyond the syllabus. This she did straight away and took it along to her lessons where it sat, open at the relevant page. As the lesson went along she was able to follow the teaching provided and to challenge herself even more deeply from the book. She started to ask many more 'why' questions, which until then she had kept to herself. Her interest grew, so too did her enjoyment. Her grades improved. Others in the class asked to use her text book.

Case study 79

Connor (year 12) was a fascinating mentee. He thought deeply and had opinions on many things. He had been told by his teachers to read around the subjects but questioned the suggestion. To him this was an enjoyable extra but surely his main focus should be to understand the syllabus and fulfil the specifications to achieve top grades. He was aiming to study accountancy as it would earn him lots of money and yet when he talked about this career objective it did not register in his eyes.

I wondered had anything enthused him recently in has studies. In fact he had been enthralled by a lesson on the philosophy of science. This, I informed him, he could study at university. He was indeed interested in philosophy but felt the potential career opportunities would not be highly paid or of interest to him. Had he looked at PPE? He had not heard of it. I sent him away to find out more.

We spent several sessions exploring course content and any specific requirements. Connor's motivation grew. This subject would allow him to pursue all his interests both those inside school and beyond, he could apply to Oxford and the career opportunities were immense. He spent time chatting to others on *The Student Room* and to current Oxbridge applicants at school. He drew up an extensive reading list for the summer. He had found inspiration.

I often find I already know what I am taught

This statement is one of a number which allow mentees to think through the reasoning behind issues they face with frustration, lack of inspiration or motivation. When I first started mentoring, pupils regularly told me that they knew quite a lot of what was taught in certain lessons. In current mentoring I find that this is much less common and almost never cited as an issue. Short-term recapping is announced as such and pupils are often asked for their input. There can be an issue when a pupil changes school or starts sixth-form. Pupils sometimes switch off as they have already covered this learning but it can then mean they are unprepared when the material and often the depth and pace change after a week or two. Quite a number of my year 12 mentees have been floored when this has happened and anxiety has set in. We discuss the fact that recapping is necessary and I encourage them to take the initiative and use the opportunity to look deeper into the subject, to ask big questions and to make clear links with other learning. Ultimately if recapping continues for a long time I encourage them to ask the teacher to suggest how they can personally take their learning forward. When learning becomes more challenging, on-going dialogue with the teacher is essential if they suffer undue stress (see Connor's story in the section on stress).

What could you teach us?

'This is a hypothetical question, it will not happen. One day you come to school and for whatever reason a class or group of pupils does not have a teacher but your tutor says "That does not matter, X is really good at ..., he/she can teach them." What would you feel confident to teach to a group of pupils? It could be a specific area of a school subject or a skill or knowledge you have acquired in your own time. Be precise!'

When I ask this question mentees gasp and often laugh. There are times when I can almost see the brains of some mentees whirring as they excitedly consider what answer to give. Others are quite serious whilst a few look panic-stricken. For these I re-iterate that this is a hypothetical scenario and explain that I am measuring their confidence levels. The answer both illustrates confidence but also resourcefulness and ingenuity in what they would choose and how they would do it. It also indicates their willingness to have a go, to act alone. For some it is also a spring board to tell me about what they have already done. At times we are able to use the skill they have identified to increase their involvement in school life or to grow inspiration. Occasionally mentees struggle to think of anything or describe a very vague scenario. This, in conjunction with their other responses, enables us to work on building their confidence further. In one school where a marked number of pupils had already told me in the previous section that if they had the choice they would like to study classical civilisation, several then indicated that they would feel confident in teaching a class with their knowledge to date. This clearly showed that not only were they interested but had done something to further this. I drew this to the attention of the school as a possible future A level choice.

Case study 80

Jordan (year 10) was a high achiever, particularly in maths. I was surprised therefore when in response to this question he said 'Intermediate or basic maths.' 'And why have you chosen this?' I enquired. 'More complex stuff would panic me I think and might lead me to doubt myself' he replied. I made a note of his response. These anxieties were highlighted during our discussion on stress (see relevant section).

Following his wonderful progress and praise from his maths teacher now that his homework was regularly in on time, I shared his comment with my link teacher. She agreed to quietly speak to his maths teacher to ask him to encourage Jordan to share his understanding with the class when more complex processes were being covered.

Case study 81

Danielle (year 13) lit up at this question and told me that she loved to set up learning opportunities with groups of friends. She had arranged a series of film nights, complete with popcorn, to enable her French class to see as many French films as possible. The previous summer, determined to do well in her AS levels, she had also got together a group of friends to share revision tips and exam strategies. Everyone had learnt from each other. Did the school know I wondered? She gave me permission to share her wonderful idea with my link teacher.

Case study 82

'What could you teach us Oliver?' Without hesitation he replied 'Computers, everything about them.' I asked him to enlighten me. Oliver (year 13) was studying ICT at A level. In addition to this he had set up his own computer business to give advice on software, repairs and hardware. He was now thinking of starting another area to teach basic lessons on how to use computers effectively in big business. This insight was extremely helpful to me.

Oliver was not achieving highly at school. He found the course requirements of his A levels tedious and far too theoretical. However, in his outside life he was highly inquisitive and creative. He regularly applied what he had learnt in real life situations both in his on-line business and in his job at an outdoor venture shop. The school was unaware of his initiative. Read his story in the section on big questions to see what happened next.

Reflectiveness

Many gifted pupils have a remarkable propensity for deep thought, producing 'big' questions and wonderful insights. However, far too often I find that they do not exercise this ability. Mentees tell me that they do not have sufficient time and feel this is unnecessary to achieve their target grades. Sadly some have even asked me why teachers cover anything that is not in the syllabus. We have had some really interesting discussions on the value of education. More than anything else I emphasise the enjoyment gained from studying in depth and breadth and also the deepening of understanding when links are made within and between subjects. This often enables more speedy and effective learning, essential for the highest results. This reflexion is inextricably linked to inspiration.

I have good ideas

The white page syndrome is very much the symbol of ideas for gifted young people. Many have wonderful, innovative, creative ideas, in fact so many that they struggle to get them all down before they disappear or to choose between them, the paper is too limiting. Others on the other hand struggle to come up with any ideas at all. The longer they spend thinking, the more terrifying the empty paper becomes. Initial attempts are likely to be quickly discarded, the scrunched up balls of paper being hurled across the room. Our son Noel was in the latter category. For him the answer was to request a default idea to work from and then to use us, his family, as his 'brain-storming' team to help trigger new thoughts. Constant practice was required.

Then there are those who do have good ideas but are so lacking in self-esteem or confidence that they dismiss them as not worth sharing, think so hard they convince themselves no-one will be interested or do not share them out loud so that they never realise how unique and helpful they are (see Shannon's story – 33). There is also quite a large group whose aim is to complete their work in as little time as possible or are too easily content with initial thoughts and so do not create the conditions necessary for inspiration to flow.

Case study 83
Paige (year 10) was severely dyslexic. She worked extremely hard to counter this by doing lots of preparation for essays. She showed me the format suggested by her teacher where she jotted down her ideas and then thought of key words and

good vocabulary. Using this method she could check the spellings beforehand and then commit the most useful words to memory. Her ideas were well thought out and highly creative. Her problem she told me was that in exams she became so concerned about the spellings that she lost the thread of her ideas. I introduced her to the concept of brain-dumping where she briefly jotted down all her ideas before she started to answer each question, so that they were there for reference and she did not have to worry about forgetting them. This allowed her to quickly sort through them and select and organise the ideas she had time to use in her response. She could also jot down the relevant words she had learnt so that nothing would stop the flow of her writing. Paige went away to practice against the clock.

Case study 84

Jordan (year 10) was excellent at maths and highly logical. He really struggled however with creative thinking. I had the opportunity to see him taking part in an inter-school questioning workshop. At one point pupils were required in small groups to think of excellent 'fat' questions they could ask in response to a picture stimulus. At first pupils' involvement was hesitant and their contributions limited. Then the suggestion of one group member created a snowball effect of responses. Pupils were fully in the flow and the resulting group question they decided upon was fascinating.

At our next mentoring session I asked Jordan to talk me through his experience. He admitted that initially he was intimidated by the thought of sharing ideas with relative strangers as he was concerned what they would think. He struggled to come up with anything very deep. It was hard work. However, once someone had a good idea, he was amazed how much this helped him to think of one himself. He was buzzing! Jordan realised that he had the ability for innovative thought, he just needed to create the right environment. As a target I asked him to involve himself in group discussion to build his own ideas and responses.

At the following session he told me that he had been discussing animal testing and cloning with his friends. In fact this had led to him changing his views. I encouraged him to keep on going, assuring him that the more he took part in such activities and opened his mind to new ideas the better he would become at creating and developing his own.

Case study 85

Callum (year 10) asked to focus on ideas. As he put it 'I get stuck on ideas.' When he was answering questions in English or RE for instance he often found it difficult to think of more than one point, however, in engineering this was easy as he used logic. I asked what techniques he currently used. He explained that he stuck with it for about ten minutes and then tried sleeping on it, which often helped him. Sometimes he also spoke to other people. We talked through using a logical approach to help him find answers and working through the basic Who, What, Why, When and How structure and the need to stick with the question for longer.

Callum said he struggled most in exams. What should he do? Between us we came up with looking back at his points so far, breaking down the title, having a secret break and visualising previous discussions. He was intrigued by the idea of a secret break. How would this be possible? No, he could not leave the room but I suggested he could close his eyes and in his mind imagine himself at home taking a break and doing whatever he did then. This temporary distraction from the exam question would hopefully give him the concentration break he needed to provide inspiration. I wondered if he had any tests in the next few days. He had an RE test so I set him the target of taking a secret break and assessing how it helped.

When we next met Callum told me he had forgotten to use the technique in RE. He often forgot targets. However, he had used it when doing his Italian homework and found it worked well. In so doing he had realised how noisy it was in the dining room where he worked and so was now talking to his Mum to see if he could have a table in his bedroom which he could use when his brother was not in there. It was good to see that Callum was adopting a more reflective, pro-active approach. We had previously discussed the value of focussed, regular piano practice when talking about learning from mistakes (case study 19). I encouraged him to adopt the same idea of regular practice with this technique as this would bring the greatest success.

Case study 86

Rachel (year 13) was a delightful mentee with no family history of going on to further education. She greatly enjoyed graphics but often found that her inspiration was limited and ideas did not flow until too near deadlines to enable her to pursue them. This year she had a new teacher who set her the challenge to create at least 20 thumbnail sketches to explore the current theme. Rachel was unsure about this but started to sketch. When she came to see me she had already completed 20 and I challenged her to see how many more she could create. By the next time we met she had completed 35 and chosen two to experiment with, finally deciding on one which she was now developing. She proudly showed me her designs and talked me through her ideas. The process had forced her to expand her ideas and in so doing enabled her to see the depths of which she was capable in a surprisingly short timescale. Rachel achieved a much better outcome then would otherwise have been the case. I encouraged her to bring along her work each time and to talk me through her progress. She enjoyed having another sounding board with whom to bounce ideas around and to talk them through, one not involved in design. Our regular conversations also gave her an accountability ensuring that the ideas stage was fully completed in good time.

Learning is sufficiently deep and broad

In conversation many mentees tell me that learning, at times, is neither sufficiently deep nor broad enough for them, by which they mean it usually does not go beyond the syllabus. As one mentee told me 'At GCSE if we asked deeper questions some teachers told us we did not need to know that as it was not on the syllabus.' Some choose to disregard this limitation and research further themselves dependent on their interest, need to understand fully or desire to place their learning in context. Others however feel that although it may be useful and rewarding, their study load does not permit them this luxury. Rarely do mentees choose to highlight any limitations under this section as in the context of specification requirements they are adequately catered for. However, this topic is often addressed under frustration, interesting learning, inspiration and asking big questions. Please see those sections for further details.

Case study 87

Michael (year 9) was a highly confidant mentee. He achieved well but did not seem greatly interested in his subjects or study in general. This was in keeping with the self-image I realised he liked to project. He was a 'popular' boy. His main interest was sport. In our second session, seeking to increase his motivation and effort in a discussion about the depth and breadth of his learning, I asked him what he was currently studying in geography, his favourite subject. He briefly talked about a certain area of Britain. I enquired if he was interested in finding out more for himself. Yes he was but there just was not time with all his homework. I asked if he had a computer at home. 'Well, Yes!' he replied. I wondered if he ever looked up extra details to go a bit deeper or broader. 'I think it would be interesting,' he continued 'but I have too much homework to fit it in.' I enquired if he had a Facebook account. He did. I told him that when I popped in to speak to my children whilst they were doing their homework I often saw them quickly click off Facebook and onto their homework task. They told me that they briefly did this whilst they were waiting for files to load or thinking things through. Concentration on homework provided time for friends to reply to their posts. This raised a smile from Michael. I suggested that his next target should be to find out some interesting additional facts about this area in between his Facebook posts.

At our next session Michael recounted some fascinating information. How long had it taken him I wondered? In fact very little and it had not interfered with his Facebook activity. He grinned as he realised the point I was making. We tried the same target again but this time using other sites and his text book. Michael began to understand how much you could find out in a relatively short time and in fact how interesting and worthwhile this was. I challenged him to share his findings with his teacher. This was not easy as he did not want to be seen speaking to the teacher but we discussed how and where this would be possible. Gradually he travelled deeper into his geography studies.

I have a good memory

Up to GCSE many gifted pupils tell me that they have a good memory. Their recall of facts, explanations, vocabulary, equations is excellent, often involving virtually no effort. Some appear to have a photographic memory. In the sixth form a very different picture emerges. The level and volume of study is challenging and frequently mentees attest to a poor memory. They find, often for the first time, that they need to put time and effort into memorising learning and, not having developed previous strategies, they struggle. Some feel guilty as they believe that a gifted pupil should not have to work hard to memorise learning, this does not fit with their picture of themselves. In fact what they are experiencing is not an inability but merely a lack of strategies. Their struggle can be overcome, they just need to learn how, to be prepared to discover methods that work for them and then to put in time to master these techniques. They require reflectiveness, resourcefulness and resilience. This process is not a quick fix.

There are of course some mentees whose memory is not as good as they would like and who have to work hard to improve it, these include those with additional learning needs such as dyslexia and some exceptionally gifted pupils who are so engrossed in deep thought that they require prompts to aid memory. As one successful Oxbridge applicant told me, 'I remember the seemingly unimportant as I am working to a bigger script.' He had learnt to compensate by extensive use of written memos and post-it notes with useful quotes about the house. Often those with additional needs are the mentees who make the most progress as they are used to struggle and willing to reflect and find ways forward.

I have regularly used the chapter on memory in Stella Cottrell's book *The study skills handbook* working through the exercises at the beginning of the chapter with mentees and then asking them to read the rest to select a few strategies to try out for themselves. Tony Buzan's books on Mind Maps are also very useful. Some of their favourite methods have been colour-coding to aid revision and help with grouping of verbs in language learning, post-it notes on the bedroom wall and around the house to aid memorisation of vocabulary and keywords, the use of a tablet to learn law cases on the college run, mentally replaying class discussions to recall differing arguments in law, politics and biology. Strategies are also featured in the chapters on making links.

Case study 88

Bethany (year 13) highlighted her memory as poor. When I asked her to talk me through why she thought this, she explained that she only achieved well in exams when she revised, otherwise her memory was not instantaneous. I reassured her that this was quite normal and in fact the very point of revision. It was the clever thing to do to achieve the task in hand and not a sign of a poor memory. I asked her what techniques she used. Bethany was highly artistic so had incorporated these skills into her revision methods. She highlighted her condensed notes, written on big sheets of paper on her bedroom wall, and then visualised them. She also used home-made notes using different types of paper, colours and shapes which she stuck around her mirror. These provided multiple visual prompts. I was delighted to be able to tell Bethany that she certainly did not have a poor memory and that her creativity in finding strategies that worked for her was one which many pupils would benefit from emulating.

Case study 89

Kieran (year 13) always looked at the floor as he spoke and constantly played with his pen. He was struggling in the sixth form and had convinced himself that no-one could help. He gave memory a low score. It had been ok at GCSE he said as he had not needed to revise. The fact that he now did added to his low opinion of himself. He was struggling to do so effectively. I asked him to show me an example of something he could not master. He pulled his biology textbook from his bag and leaved through to a complex diagram. Not being a scientist, I asked him to talk me through what it showed. He looked up, sighed and told me he really did not know. He added that he was the only person in his class who was not doing chemistry as well and this really hampered his understanding. I shared how difficult, if not impossible, I would find it to memorise something which I did not understand and so could not find a way to link to the other learning in my brain. He looked quizzical. First, I continued, he had to talk it through with someone to make it accessible. He mentioned that he had already booked a session with his teacher to talk through his performance. I encouraged him to address his lack of understanding.

At our next session Kieran told me that the meeting with his teacher had gone well. He had reassured him and given him an overview of his learning. This, with an explanation of the diagram, had greatly helped. We looked at memory techniques using *The study skills handbook*. Kieran chose revising out loud. I did not see Kieran for more than a month due to extra school activities and the Easter holiday. This time he was much more smiley. He was still not great at memory but now that he understood the material better he was making much better progress. He was helping himself by doing extra questions in his text book and rereading sections out loud when necessary. Kieran had begun to realise that ability is not fixed and that he had a part to play. It was up to him to figure out how best to accomplish that role.

Case study 90

Ellie (year 12) was a highly reflective mentee. In our sessions we used the learning person diagram (see Three really useful diagrams) together with her responses to the questionnaire to determine our focus. Ellie particularly wanted to build her confidence. We talked through her subjects, one by one, considering how she might do this. Ellie told me that she felt great stress in the lead up to exams as she always worried that she had not done enough. For her January mock in biology, so decided to spend time creating revision cards.

At our next session Ellie brought along a few of her revision cards to show me. She had condensed the information on each page of her revision guide onto a card. She said that as she was going along she was getting much better at selecting the right information to feature and being much more precise. She carried them around with her to read when she had a few minutes. Her plan was to test herself and if she understood the concept to put the card to one side. The next stage, she had decided, was to explain to her Dad the title of the card. He was not a biologist so she would need to be really clear. In her exam a primary focus would be the quality and clarity of her written communication so this method would ensure she achieved this. Ellie's method with regular reviews and the use of her Dad to test her understanding gradually prepared her to take her exam with confidence. Her teacher was so impressed that he used her as an example of best practice across the department.

I have regularly used her story both to help mentees adopt a structured approach to revision and to show parents who feel their child is much more knowledgeable than them, how to usefully support their learning.

Case study 91

Anna (year 10) took away the ideas from Stella Cottrell's book to read with interest. As always, she tried a few techniques and used these as a springboard to create her own. At the following session I was fascinated to hear her ideas. As a keen sports person she had decided to incorporate sport into her revision schedule. She was struggling with remembering the many facts covered in biology. Her sister had taken this to A level. After some discussions to build her understanding they had decided to use their games of tennis to make testing fun.

As they went through a knock about, her sister would call out a question as the ball left her racket and Anna would answer as it left hers, either immediately or when the rhythm of play had given her time to think. They also did the same when playing Frisbee. Not only did this make the experience fun and speed up her recall but Anna found her visual memory of these moments provided an additional aid to recall.

Anna reflected on the idea of experiential aide and this lead to a new technique. She quietly played a different song in the background when revising different topics and by running through the song in her mind she found she could then better remember what she had learnt.

She also found the traditional technique of reading through her learning and asking her mum to test her was highly beneficial as her mum always brought out the best in her and her patience and kindness helped her adopt a can-do attitude which greatly aided her memory.

Case study 92
Paige (year 10) found that she needed lots of visual clues to help her remember keywords and also constant reminders. I told her about our daughter Lydia's technique of putting post-it notes around the house with vocabulary or key facts. Some were even in the tea cupboard or on the back of the loo door. Paige thought this was a wonderful idea but assured me her mother would not allow her to do so. We talked through the possibilities of her bedroom. She decided to stick them on the side of her wardrobe using different colours for different things and grouping them to aid memory. This proved to be highly successful and Paige's mother was delighted to see the impact of the technique.

The style of teaching and learning suits me

Nowadays most schools address the concept of learning styles and many mentees respond to this question with regard to what they know about themselves as visual, aural or kinaesthetic learners. Many are also aware that at different times and for different tasks we need to use different styles. Indeed, the flexibility required often requires a level of resilience which is most helpful to the pupil. Usually by year 10, pupils have had opportunities to develop this skill.

This question also refers to the style of teaching and learning in the broadest sense. Mentees sometimes find the overall style too limiting, not allowing them to adopt their own methodology, do their own research or develop themselves sufficiently as a learner, thus limiting their reflectiveness and problem-solving ability. An example of this is Jake's story in the section on frustration and Harry's story in the section on praise. Other reflections are contained in the section on – How could we make school/learning even better?

Case study 93
Zoe (year 13) had scored this question as a two. We talked through all her responses, unpicking the thought behind them. When we came to this question she thought for a while and then explained.

'In lessons there is just not enough space to think. I like to be taught and then have time to read and think about what I have learnt to embed it before I start to do exercises. Teachers usually expect you to go straight into examples and I panic and make mistakes. There isn't always enough time at home afterwards to sort this out.' Another of my mentees from a different school had recently voiced the same idea. Zoe seemed pleased to hear she was not unique but rejected my suggestion she talk to the teacher out of class to ask if space could be made available, perhaps occasionally. She was too shy and having been one of the few to achieve highly at her secondary school, she found it particularly hard to accept that her ideas could also help others and were worth sharing.

I emailed my school/college links to say that this idea had been suggested. They were delighted to receive the suggestion and undertook to mention it at the next staff meeting.

Case study 94

Emily (year 10) enjoyed the opportunity to find out for herself, to be in charge of her own learning. We had found ways to include this in her targets. I mentored at her school as part of a larger programme. At the end of the summer term I set all the year 10s a university project. They were each allocated a top university from the Guardian league table and requested to order or download a prospectus. Over the holiday they had to produce an interesting project in response to a series of prompt questions covering all aspects of the university package. Emily rose to the challenge. She thought hard about what people would find 'interesting' and decided to make a film focussing on the accommodation and clubs and societies on offer at her designated university. The resulting submission was highly informative, yet fun and well received by adults and pupils. She had learnt a lot and being enabled to use her own innovative and creative approach had greatly enjoyed the experience.

I see how learning in class fits together

I know how individual subjects fit the big picture

In conversation with my highest achieving and most fulfilled mentees, I have discovered that the two skills above are key to their success and the enjoyment of their studies. Not only do these skills enable them to play with their learning and make sense of it, to master it, but they engender some really big questions and allow them to make independent progress. Bite-sized learning frustrates them. Having the big picture is also extremely helpful as an aid to memory, as one idea links and gives rise to another so there is no need to learn each idea in isolation.

Too many mentees, though gifted, do not make full use of this technique. These statements allow them to reflect on their learning pattern and to assess their performance subject by subject. Most score fairly well but a significant number put themselves in the middle. At times they see the big picture but not at others. Often this is due to passive learning. This is something they can address themselves (see Anna's story under stress) or by enlisting the support of their teachers.

Case study 95

William, year 13, performed very highly. I asked him if he would share with me some of his secrets to success so that I could use them for the benefit of others. He explained that after learning a new topic he read through his notes again and again, making links with previous learning as he went. He applied this principle during exams as well. At this point he spent days reading slowly through the entire text book several times and making links. When he had finished he had a clear picture in his mind against which to set exam questions. I have used his story with other mentees, suggesting that the picture is then transferred to paper, put up in a prominent place and regularly reviewed.

How could we make school/learning even better?

'Now, I would like you to consider what one thing you think the school could do to make your learning experience even better.'

(If they are unable to think of anything) – 'Please tell me what you think is the best thing about learning at this school.'

After considering various characteristics of a learner and a gifted pupil, and completing the section on reflection this question allows mentees to consider how their thoughts could best be applied by the school to improve their personal learning journey. Certain responses are given again and again; more practical, fun, hands-on learning to enable pupils to practice what they have learnt, a greater variety of teaching methods, more learning less teaching, greater links with real life, smaller groups/classes, more class discussion, more independent learning. There are always a number of highly insightful, individual suggestions as well. The responses have two functions. I share the overall findings with my link teacher to feed into school improvement using pupil voice. This occasionally also highlights particular trends to be addressed. Secondly, the response given can often be addressed by the mentee themselves, which helps them become more pro-active and independent. For instance I have often used Chris' mind map (see the section on distractions) to help pupils who ask for smaller classes to think through how they can help themselves instead of being too reliant on teacher support.

Case study 96

In response to my question Matthew, year 10, told me that some teachers just talked at the class. He found this very uninspiring and boring. I enquired how often this happened. He talked through his different subjects describing how each lesson worked. Some lessons were fine and some had a lot of talking but the content was made interesting or other resources were used such as PowerPoints. However, in geography the teacher generally taught from the book and then set questions. He found it really difficult to engage. He had, unusually, just had a great lesson where the teacher had used different biscuits to represent the variety of the world's resources. This was great fun and made it much easier to remember the information. Sadly though they then had to do questions from the book. What would he have done I wondered? He pondered a moment. His suggestion was to get the pupils to discuss how they could help countries with less resources improve their quality of life. The homework could then have been to formulate a list of imports and exports. I told him that teachers, like pupils, love praise and encouragement. If he liked that style of lesson and found it helped him learn then he needed to let the teacher know. We formulated a target for him to tell the teacher how much he had enjoyed the lesson.

When he came next time I enquired how this strategy had worked. Matthew answered that the teacher had thanked him for his vote of appreciation and continued that the next lesson was good as well. They looked at graphs depicting the import and export trends in differing countries and had a good class discussion. Matthew was pleased to find that he could play an important active role in influencing the style of his lessons. I followed this session up by emailing my link teacher to tell her how much one of my mentees had enjoyed a certain lesson and why. This email was then circulated further highlighting this example of excellent teaching practice.

Reciprocity

Many gifted young people thrive on the interchange of ideas with other pupils and with adults. This helps develop their thinking and greatly increases their motivation and inspiration. Some however are hampered by social isolation, limiting group dynamics or a lack of confidence. Discovering and addressing the cause is essential to enable them both to develop their own potential and to allow other learners to benefit from their insights, questions and enthusiasm for learning.

Pupils are kind at school

I have a good group of friends

Across the years I have mentored pupils aged six to eighteen and have always included a 'bullying' question to check on their emotional wellbeing in the social context of the school. Gifted pupils can be highly sensitive, more mature than others their age and feel very different and at times as though they do not belong. This is sometimes made worse by the policy in some schools of sending these pupils on external G and T courses without then working with them to cascade the learning so that all pupils benefit. Sadly this can lead to the charge of elitism firstly by the parents of their classmates and then by their classmates themselves, ultimately causing this valuable life-line to sometimes be rejected. It is on these courses that pupils have the opportunity to meet others like them in learning needs but also working at their level or beyond. For some pupils this is a rare opportunity to be challenged.

By the time they reach year 10, however, pupils have usually found their niche and the pupil body are generally accepting of individual interests and ability. In the schools where I have mentored, where there is a culture of high achievement in all areas, celebration of all abilities and an effective anti-bullying policy, pupils normally feel able to be themselves and to achieve at the level of which they are able. The mentoring sessions help pupils to understand and accept themselves, which in turn increases their confidence and self-esteem. Generally, I have found that it is only the occasional pupil, perhaps with other needs such as dyslexia or mental health issues or with additional family needs, who tells me that pupils are not kind. This information is shared with my school link.

I am delighted to find that by year 10 almost all pupils tell me that they have a good group of friends. This social element is essential for them to function well in society and avoid becoming withdrawn. For some developing good friendships has happened naturally through tighter ability setting in GCSE years, allowing them to make new friends and through subject choice so that they are more often in a class of pupils who share their passion. Others have begun to realise that they need to have different friends for different things. This allows them to address their range of interests with different groups of people depending on whether they wish to make music, discuss Shakespeare or play Frisbee. Many choose to have some older friends allowing them to share their thoughts on a higher level. Opportunities to do so often exist within school clubs, county music/sport groups or scout/guide groups for example. Mentees often greatly enjoy the opportunity to meet other mentees, both across their own school or as part of inter-school activities. Some also choose to become part of on-line communities like IGGY, an on-line forum for international gifted young people.

A small number, particularly the under-achiever, need guidance and support to broaden their friendships, allowing them to spend more time with pupils of similar ability who have discovered a love of learning. Discussions in mentoring sessions allow this to be handled sensitively and for potential concerns to be carefully addressed.

Case study 97
Ryan (year 10) was under-achieving in many of his subjects. The school informed me he was part of a friendship group where hard work was not a top priority. Ryan elucidated further. He did not belong to school clubs and certainly did not put himself forward for occasional volunteer roles.

Whilst talking about his passions Ryan told me that he liked exploring computer programs, an interest he had acquired from his Dad. He also liked to build 'stuff.' At home he read extensively about how to design apps, programs and games. I talked to my link teacher about this.

The school was in the process of revamping its extra-curricular programme. The link contact asked Ryan and a few other selected pupils about the feasibility of setting up a computer club for programming or design. The opportunity to work on real life applications greatly appealed to him. It was also decided to ask the Engineering Development Trust for help in finding a STEM (science, technology, engineering and maths) ambassador to come and work with the group. Ryan attended the first session. He came away buzzing with possibilities. His confidence and enthusiasm grew in leaps and bounds. He started to meet with some of the club members occasionally out of club sessions to discuss on-going designs. He was making new friends and doing a 'cool' activity.

I enjoy learning in a group

The concept of group learning is greatly welcomed by nearly all gifted mentees. The opportunity to work with others to explore and pool ideas, share skills and build confidence is seen as highly positive; facilitating exciting conversations with lots of interaction and leading to better solutions. When groups work well there is a real buzz. Much learning takes place.

However, mentees offer a number of provisos to optimise the group learning experience. The composition of the group is very important. Some feel it is essential that they are grouped with people they know and like as this increases their confidence and maximises their involvement. Some prefer to be with people they do not know as this limits distractions. Jordan's story in the section on I have good ideas, illustrates the power of working with unknown pupils as a tool to unleashing previously un-experienced levels of thought. In a very large group another possible strategy is offered in Shannon's story in the section on confidence.

It is also essential that ground rules are set so that no-one is excluded or ridiculed and that everyone is expected to fully participate. Many get frustrated by pupils who waste time or do nothing and sadly therefore the gifted pupils fail to benefit fully from such opportunities.

The content and level of discussion is also highly important. As one mentee told me 'When the task is riveting, group work is really stimulating. I love it.' Some of my most gifted mentees tell me they prefer independent study as then much deeper thought takes place and a better outcome is achieved. One year 13 emphatically told me that she was an independent learner and so did not enjoy these opportunities. It is important that pupils see group learning as a complimentary tool to their individual learning.

In addition some mentees have wonderful ideas and very clear opinions on how they should be achieved. They do not want their idea to be lost. They often feel group working limits these and the final outcome is compromised.

Group-working is a vital transferable skill so it is essential that pupils learn to positively take part. In order to optimise their experience and build their levels of resilience, resourcefulness, reflectiveness and reciprocity the provision of opportunities to work at times with other gifted pupils, whether in school or beyond, is highly beneficial both socially and in challenging their learning.

I talk about my learning with my teachers

Dialogue is highly beneficial to gifted pupils. The ability not only to understand but to master their learning depends on it. Those who go beyond basic clarification, seek to address any areas of weakness and then delve deeper into their learning, sharing their fascination for a subject, voicing their insights, connections and conundrums develop a deep love for learning. Their passion shines through whether in class, on their personal statement or in interview. They will be the inventors, entrepreneurs, great thinkers of tomorrow. Why then do some pupils find it so difficult to talk to their teachers?

Peer pressure may inhibit pupils but as they progress through the school many more engage in dialogue and by the sixth form this is much more common. Many are too passive, particularly in years 10 and 11, and do not appreciate that they need to be a partner in their own learning (this can be more marked in those from disadvantaged backgrounds). Passivity may be compounded by low self-esteem and shyness. A significant number are embarrassed or feel guilty when they do not understand something and, assuming that everyone else does and believing they should too, neither ask questions nor share insights. Some experience great anxiety at the idea of speaking to teachers and so avoid this activity whenever possible, even though this leads to major frustration when they subsequently feel unable to take their learning further. Sadly some are put off by their initial experiences when certain teachers do not respond in a positive manner or no time is available for pupil/teacher discussion.

Often issues faced by mentees have been addressed by speaking to a teacher; to improve as a learner, to solve subject difficulties and to take their learning forward. The benefits have been many; progress and fulfilment by the mentee, improved learning for classmates and great enjoyment for the teacher who has the opportunity to talk about a subject they love. Mastery of the art of adult dialogue equips the gifted pupil for future study and research.

There are many illustrations of the impact of teacher dialogue throughout this book: Megan - I feel good about myself, Anna – I never feel stressed, Connor – I am sensitive, Rebecca – I am confident, Harry –Teachers often praise my learning, Alice – I get frustrated by the learning at school.

Case study 98
Samantha (year 13) a vivacious, deep-thinking mentee from a disadvantaged background, rated the inspiration gained from her learning as one and the

regularity with which she talked about her learning with her teachers as a two. I asked her to explain to me why she had given inspiration such a low score. In her opinion she felt A levels were naturally uninspiring and specifications were dull. She added that she would not feel right talking to her teacher to increase her inspiration. This was not something she had ever done. However, she was fascinated by her research into the placebo effect and its place in modern medicine in which she was engaged for her EPQ.

A few sessions later, when we had made some progress in addressing other issues, I suggested that she talk to one of her teachers about something in which she was really interested. This she thought would be either in biology or psychology. When she came next she told me that she had spoken to the biology teacher about her interest in the function of the kidneys and also about how memories are formed. I wondered how she had found the experience. 'It was good' she said, 'and the teacher was surprised at the depth of my knowledge.'

Shortly after this Samantha started to query her decision to study medicine at university. She loved the idea of research and the huge amount of choice open to a biology student. She realised it was biology that truly inspired her. Ultimately she rejected her medicine place and chose her fifth choice, biology. Her conversation with her teacher had been pivotal in helping her see where her true interests lay.

Case study 99
Our son Noel in year 13 was struggling to understand one of his physics topics. I suggested he talk to his teacher. He did not. He was too anxious and felt embarrassed. At the following parents' evening the teacher queried why Noel was no longer joining in class discussion. I mentioned Noel's anxiety and explained that he assumed everyone else understood so he would look stupid asking for clarification. She was extremely shocked and told him that he was one of her best pupils. If he did not understand then there was little hope for his classmates. Furthermore, his questions were highly valuable to the class dynamics. It was these which drove the discussion and engendered additional queries and insights. As an encouragement she told him the story of Simon. He was a few years older than Noel and loved physics. He regularly came to ask her to explain things. He would often return on several occasions to ask her to re-explain. He was determined to fully understand. Far from being cross or annoyed she was delighted that he was so interested in his studies. He went on to study at Imperial College and then did a PhD.

This story did the trick. Noel regained the confidence to ask questions. Dynamic class discussions resumed. I have successfully used this story many times with mentees to help them see the value of talking to their teachers and to understand that the inability to understand a concept immediately is not a failing but a valuable learning opportunity.

What have you learnt from other pupils?

'The reason for asking this question is that I once mentored a gifted boy in year 6 at a school where I was the gifted and talented governor. This school had just decided to stop setting pupils in English although it still continued to do so in maths. They recognised that even though some pupils had difficulty writing or spelling, their ideas often inspired others, leading to higher achievement by all. This boy was horrified by the idea. He just could not believe that he could learn from those he saw as less clever than himself. I found this very sad. With this attitude he was destined to miss out greatly in life.

Tell me about a time you learnt something from someone your own age or maybe older or younger but not a teacher. It could be recently or long ago.'

Mentees are often intrigued by this question and take a while to come up with an answer. Sometimes it is fairly unimaginative, at others it is highly creative and insightful. We do not spend a long time on the response but it is useful for them to have the opportunity to consider the value of learning from others. To date I have not encountered a mentee who has never learnt from another pupil. At least, none have admitted to this but the question has undoubtedly got them thinking.

Time and again pupils have attested to the benefit of learning from others and asking an expert. Many have told me how helpful it has been to have had something explained by a friend who knows them and can reword an explanation, previously given by a teacher, so that they understand perfectly. Ideas and insights gained during group revision sessions in class have helped. Many have also learnt useful learning tips from older pupils or class mates, often another way of thinking or doing something such as note-taking, or essay writing or perhaps more general tips on time management. Some have benefitted more from life or social skills such as coping with friendship problems, being more patient, learning to relax more and not constantly to think about work. One year 10 told me he had learnt 'Not to waste this period of your life.'

An example of asking an expert is Josh's story under – What subjects are you studying? Danielle's formulation of a study group to learn from each other's methods features in – What could you teach us?

Other Factors

As a mentor I have the privileged gift of time to talk 1:1 which is so often in short supply in the school environment. This gives me the opportunity to ask questions to allow a holistic diagnosis of the mentee's needs. These 'other factors' often hold an important piece of the jigsaw and yet are rarely asked in school. They are of a more personal nature and I always preface the section with the statement that mentees may choose not to answer if they wish. To date none have. In fact the responses are regularly very open and deep. Pupils want to talk. At the end of one group session where I was working through the questionnaire with a year 8 cohort of G and T pupils, I asked for any particular lessons they had learnt or insights they had gained from the process. One boy commented that he had not thought before about the impact of sleep levels, diet, exercise and family and friends on his learning. He now saw how important they were.

Do you have enough sleep?

Mentees vary in their concept of enough sleep. The amount itself is not as important as their view of whether they consider it sufficient to allow them to learn well at school and during personal study time. For some too little sleep is a concern, for others too much which still leaves them exhausted. Asking this question has brought to light a number of important issues that may not otherwise have been voiced until later, if at all. Talking through the reasons for too much or too little sleep, mentees have admitted, amongst other issues, to anxiety over a lack of understanding, excessive homework leading to very late nights, perfectionism resulting in extended homework sessions (see Emma's story – Perfectionism), a chronic inability to manage distractions (Jordan's story – Stress) and, on a more positive note, problems trying to silence a mind buzzing with ideas. They have also mentioned issues relating to family circumstances, mental health and medical conditions. Talking through these concerns has enabled me to signpost to other relevant agencies. Several older pupils gained encouragement to persevere with investigations at the doctors and to speak to school staff about their health. This lead to one applying for extenuating circumstances due to the effects of illness when taking her A levels. Finally, the demands of part-time work, particularly the early hours required by the paper round or the ever-increasing hours of the flexible weekend job adversely account for limited sleep.

Do you have a balanced diet?

Virtually all my mentees tell me they eat a balanced diet although a few admit they should eat more fruit or vegetables. Posing the question allows them to consider the impact of their diet and how to address any issues. On occasion I have encountered a mentee whose poor diet is linked to low family income. This I have shared with the school link.

Do you drink enough water?

Mentees understand the need for adequate fluid but a significant number do not drink enough. Some do not like water but do drink other types of non-carbonated fluids, although these may contain excessive caffeine.

Do you do regular exercise?

Most mentees do regular exercise. Some initially say they do not as they see exercise as going to the gym, cycling, playing sport or belonging to a dance class. However, when asked if they walk to school, quite a number tell me they have a journey of more than 30 minutes, which I count as regular exercise. Most of those doing paper rounds instance this as a form of exercise but some need reminding.

Case study 100

Alexander (year 12) chose to focus on sleep. He slept well but not for long enough. Indeed, he could not stop yawning! We talked about the reasons. He had now transferred to college which started later than school. As his younger siblings still started early he was constantly woken by them in the mornings. Could he not go to sleep earlier I wondered? It transpired that he went to bed in good time but played on his phone and then was constantly disturbed by texts. What could he do about this? With encouragement he thought he could charge it elsewhere. He did not want to chat to his friends during the night. His target was to charge it downstairs and report back on his success and the impact of his strategy. He slept longer but still was not fully rested. I suggested he go to bed earlier and get up at the same time as his siblings so he did not start the day annoyed and was better able to engage with his learning. He did not like this idea. We moved onto other targets.

Several sessions later Alexander arrived at our session wide awake and much more responsive. I enquired what had happened. He was now getting up earlier so that he had an hour before leaving for college. How had he managed this I wondered? He had asked his mother to ensure he did. She had started to cook him breakfast. It would be rude not to eat it he added. Alexander's engagement improved significantly.

Case study 101

Zoe (year 13) highlighted lack of sleep as an issue. She told me that it took her a long time to unwind at night. I asked if she knew why this was. Zoe worked late at her job. Where did she work and how many hours did she do? To my amazement, she told me that although she was contracted for 12 hours at the supermarket where she worked she did 30 to 36 hours a week. They regularly asked her to do overtime and she did not want to let them down. I told her that she needed to decide whether she wanted a career in the supermarket industry or whether she wanted to access the university course she told me was her aim. Although the supermarket valued her as a hard worker they were truly not interested in her as a person but as a pair of hands. She commented that her mum and dad were becoming annoyed at the amount of ferrying around they were having to do. I asked her to go away and think what sort of future she would like. She needed to choose.

Concerned by what Zoe had told me I went to see my college contact. He confirmed that the college recommended a limit of 12 hours for part-time work alongside full-time study. He had met Zoe's parents at parents' evening and knew they were highly supportive. They had not been to university themselves but were keen to help Zoe achieve her dream to do so. He would speak to them.

At our next session Zoe informed me that she had decreased her hours to 12 as her mock exams were approaching. She had been scared to tell her boss but spoke to a different staff member. I suggested she did not exceed this level in future. Her parents had become more strict and turned the internet off at 10pm. She was focussed on her studies.

Zoe did not do as well as she had hoped in her exams but realising this could be remedied with concerted effort, retook several exams in the summer whilst studying hard for her new ones. She did not increase her work hours and gained a place at her chosen university.

Case study 102

Natasha (year 13) arrived looking like a ghost. She answered all the questions but seemed extremely vague and several times told me how boring she found her studies. She had been told she had underachieved at GCSE and had not done very well at AS. When we came to 'Other factors' she told me that she rarely managed to get to sleep before three in the morning, drank about a cup of water a day and did not do any exercise. I was most concerned and informed my school link.

At our next session I decided to focus on these factors. Success in these areas was critical to help her go forwards. Our first target was for her to carry a bottle of water around with her and have a sip at the start of every lesson. I also asked her to find out what interesting exercise opportunities were available where she lived. In the meantime we looked at her school timetable and started to discuss how she could use the study periods more effectively to help build her interest. There was plenty of time after homework left for more in-depth reading and posing wondering questions.

At our next session Natasha told me she had discovered a local Zumba class and had started to attend with some of her extended family. It was really good. She had also done some additional reading alongside her homework and was beginning to find school more enjoyable. Her sleep pattern was improving.

By the time I saw Natasha next, a month later due to school holidays, she told me the extra study had helped and she was feeling more relaxed, confidant and less distracted. School work was more interesting as she now understood it more. One of her teachers had even commented on how switched on she now was. We were both delighted. We spent time looking at next steps in each subject to maintain this momentum.

Do you have a quiet place to work?

Responses to this question link directly to the mentees' thoughts on the definition of quiet (see – I learn best when it is quiet). A minority preface their response with 'I do not like quiet' or 'I cannot work in quiet.' However, most pupils confirm that this facility is available at home. Several of my more disadvantaged mentees have told me of issues due to small houses and shared rooms or homework study spaces and computer stations located in the main living room. One enterprising family had acquired some headphones for their son so that he could zone out of the noise around him. Another mentee, after reflecting on this question negotiated with her parents to move bedrooms so that she was no longer above the living room. Sadly, another mentee, in order to finance a laptop that she could use in her room, told me she had taken on a part-time job which meant she missed some classes. She saw this as essential, so we used the sessions to address, where possible, the impact. I have also been told of noise issues due to the additional learning needs of certain family members. It seems rare that pupils discuss these issues with school. Asking this question starts the dialogue. A possible solution can then be found.

Do you talk through your learning at home?

Many of my mentees see talking with their parents about their learning as something to be done only when they need help. As they become more advanced, unless their parent is an expert in that particular field, this is less and less likely. Sadly, some parents to whom I have spoken at parent workshops reinforce this view. 'He is far beyond where I got at school'. 'I am not as clever as her. I left school and went straight out to work.' Both mentees and parents are missing the point. The parent plays a vital role.

Opportunities to talk about learning, as we saw in the section on 'I talk about my learning with my teachers', are highly beneficial for a pupil. The interest and support of a parent is invaluable. Parents may not have had the opportunity or encouragement to go to university themselves but this does not mean they lack the ability for meaningful dialogue. The pupil is, after all, their offspring. There are so many ways in which talking to parents can help and those mentees who avail themselves of this opportunity, making use of all available resources, are those who become the best learners.

Dialogue allows pupils to mull over an idea, share their excitement at new found learning, request clarification and support, consider other perspectives, explore content more deeply to achieve mastery and build on the life skills of their parents. See Ellie's story – I have a good memory, Megan's story – I feel good about myself and Joseph's story – I see mistakes as learning opportunities.

Some parents need support and direction. It is not always easy as a parent to know exactly in what way and how often to help, especially for those not acquainted with the demands of high level study. There are also times when the parent knows that their child needs to spend more time on study or tackle homework more in advance. The child can be far too self-assured. 'I know what I am doing!' 'I will spend more time on it later.' Sadly school effort grades that fail to acknowledge the lateness of homework or potential for even greater effort, coupled with no warning that grades may suffer leaves the parent isolated. If allowed to continue the pupil's attitude can adversely affect expected progress and achievement. Detailed advice and support from school which brings the pupil up short and perhaps includes a competitive element is extremely helpful. A good parent/school partnership is essential.

Some mentees, sadly, do not have anyone at home they can talk to. These pupils benefit enormously from mentoring sessions both to improve learning skills, address emotional and social issues and to signpost them to other experts with whom they can converse. See Danielle's story in – What could you teach us?

Do you have particular learning needs?

Do you have particular medical needs?

Do you have family/friend issues?

I am always amazed at the openness of mentees when responding to these questions. They want to share. Learning needs mentioned are generally to do with extra time allowances in certain subjects. Several are dyslexic, allowing us to build on their experience of struggle and perseverance to positively address other learning needs. See Paige's story – I have a good memory and – I have good ideas. Rarely are those on the autistic spectrum part of the mentoring programme as specialist provision is usually made enabling them to benefit from the high level of experience of the SENCO and their team.

Medical needs mentioned have accounted for extreme tiredness and stress in a number of mentees. It has been possible to support these needs emotionally and to suggest learning strategies whilst encouraging them in the ups and downs of their medical experiences.

A significant number of pupils suffer from the effects of family break up, sometimes providing an emotional bolster to at least one parent. This can lead to very low self-esteem. See Sophie's story – What are your strengths? Others have wider family issues such as bereavement, mental health problems, a senile dementia sufferer or immigration queries. Knowledge of these provides the mentee with a forum to off load and gives the mentor greater understanding when addressing learning issues, enabling a more creative approach.

At times mentees mention family issues of which the school is unaware and yet which help to account for their underachievement, such as long term absence of one parent, very recent family break-up or a child living at will between two homes. I have been able to notify the school allowing the pupils to be well supported.

Mentees generally address friendship issues under the section – I have a good group of friends and – Pupils are kind. Sometimes, however, family issues cause friendship problems leading mentees to feel particularly isolated as no one seems to understand their family limitations and this can be compounded by their different interests and outlook, which are part of their giftedness.

What would you like to gain from the mentoring sessions?

Having worked their way through the questionnaire, some mentees have a specific area they would particularly like to discuss and address. The most common ones are building confidence, increasing motivation, time management, revision techniques, organisation and setting personal targets. Some have more personal issues they wish to discuss.

As we then revisit the questionnaire, unpicking the scoring and discussing the stories behind their responses many more options for our focus materialise. They choose where to begin.

What were the benefits of mentoring?

Over the years I have mentored, I have always given pupils the chance to assess the impact of mentoring on their learning and well-being. The open atmosphere of the mentoring sessions has led them to be very frank in their assessment and appraisal. They particularly value:

- Accountability provided by the Mentor assessing their progress against targets

- The listening ear

- Talking to someone they can trust who takes them seriously and makes a note of what they say

- Time for self-reflection on personal learning techniques and motivation

- Opportunity to admit difficulties in a safe setting

- Opportunity to address underlying issues masked by success

- Realisation they are not abnormal or unique

- Tools to empower them to play an active role in their learning journey and permission to do so.

- In addition their classmates benefit from the renewed excitement and engagement of the mentee. The positive impact cascaded to other learners can be immeasurable.

- School staff have also told me they benefit from:

- Learning conversations with the mentees

- Ideas that challenge and improve their practice

- Opportunities to talk on a 1:1 basis about their subject area

- Improved class dynamics

- Big questions that take learning forward.

Giving the mentees a voice

Year 13s

'It has been nice to have someone interested in me who does not take my high achievement for granted but realises I too need help.' Charlotte

'It is good to put your learning in perspective and focus on where you are going rather than just on short term educational goals. At the end of each session I come out feeling really good.' Rinata

'It is good to have someone to build your confidence.' Emma

'I now realise that I am as good as anyone else, I always assumed pupils at private or grammar schools must be more clever.' Nicole

'Mentoring has given me the opportunity to reflect on my personal progress. Where else would I do this?' Jack

'Mentoring has helped me to structure my learning so I am now doing it in a SMARTer way.' Oliver

'Mentoring has allowed me to recognise just how much I do by allowing me to step back from what I regard as my ordinary life.' Bethany

'Mentoring has made me take more risks.' Rachel

'It has definitely made me a more confidant person by showing me that needing help is normal.' Chelsea

Year 12s

'I now know what I need to improve and where my priorities lie.' Georgia

'It is good to have someone who makes sure you keep going.' Georgia

Year 11s

'I have learnt a lot about how to make the most of my abilities.' Lucy

'I have learnt to accept that I don't always get things right and how to ask for help.' Holly

'It is really useful to talk to another person who can give you advice and who knows about learning and G and T students.' Alice

Year 10s

'I am now better at seeking advice and have improved my ability to talk to teachers.' Sarah

'Thank you for boosting my confidence.' Emily

'Mentoring has helped me with revision techniques which have helped me with all of my exams. It has also helped me to concentrate in lessons by showing me different ways in which I can learn and reflect in the lesson.' Ryan

'I hated public speaking and got nervous standing up in front of the class, however now I am able to speak with quite a bit of confidence.' Thomas

'You may think that mentoring sessions are just there to set you work. But they are there more as encouragement for you to progress with school work. They encourage you to develop your life skills such as asking questions and improving time management. They are also there to improve confidence, as they offer someone to talk to if you are having problems with school or are having a hard time with stress caused by such things as exams. One of the sacrifices of coming to these mentoring sessions is that you have to miss lessons. They might seem like vital lessons, but in truth, it is relatively easy to catch up on any work you miss. This is one of the skills that the mentoring sessions teach you as well, to go and do work outside of school to make sure that you achieve your best.' Luke

'Mentoring has made me want to find out more about what I learn in lessons and inspired a passion for discovering new things.' Shannon

'Mentoring has helped me become more confident in my school subjects and has given me the opportunity to discuss issues and come up with solutions.' Hannah

Top learning moments and tips

Learning moments for mentees

1. Gifted students make mistakes. These are a wonderful learning opportunity.

2. Gifted students sometimes will not understand their learning, they will struggle. Do not feel guilty. This does not negate the title of *gifted*. Your questions will help both you and others.

3. Struggling, coping with 'failing' and then learning to move on are a vital part of learning.

4. Hard work and revision are necessary for all pupils. This will increase as learning gets harder.

5. Ability is not determined by the speed of understanding.

6. Ability and success are not fixed, you can influence the outcome. You have a part to play. You must figure out how best to accomplish this.

7. Future success is increased if the whole person is developed. Do not cancel the rest of your life.

Tips for mentees

1. Ask an expert (in class or out and of any age) for advice when you need help with a topic, a technique, or an issue (such as stress), or get them to share their passion for a subject.

2. If you do not understand your teacher's explanation first time, keep going back. Teachers want you to succeed.

3. Take control of issues and anxieties. Be pro-active. Adopt a can-do attitude.

4. Analyse the issue. What could you do? What could the school do? Create a SMART plan.

5. Time management: Consider your workload addressing possible distractions. What would you like to achieve? What is realistic? Make a plan that fits your style of working and other commitments.

6. Divide tasks into a) must do now, b) must do but deadline is later, c) may do in the future. Each day do a) and some of b) and tackle c) over time if they are necessary.

7. Break pieces of work into manageable timed chunks.

8. Make the most of 'down' time. You will address workload more efficiently.

9. Spend time creating a mind map of how learning fits together both across and between subjects.

10. Perseverance – When you get stuck, keep going for ten more minutes, experiencing and coping with the feelings of anxiety before seeking help, if necessary.

11. Find a 'learning partner' to consider 'big' questions about different subjects.

12. Teachers enjoy talking about their subject. Share your own learning at an appropriate time.

13. When you revise, concentrate on what you do not know rather than covering the whole syllabus.

Three useful diagrams

As they have identified and addressed learning needs, considered interests, inspiration and aspiration, mentees have found it helpful to map themselves as a learner and depict their passions, interests and hobbies using these three diagrams. This then allows them to:

1. Take control of their learning, addressing weaknesses and building on strengths

2. Map their passions and build evidence

3. Map their interests and consider missing areas

The illustrations act as a valuable reminder to them once mentoring sessions have finished and provide them with a tool to plot on-going progress and plan future strategies. Pictorial mapping of these three areas has also proved very helpful to them when applying for a part-time job or completing their personal statement during the university application process. It gives them a clear structure on which to base their thoughts and writing.

Diagram 1 – Myself as a learner

Ask mentees to draw a stick person that extends from the top to the bottom of the page. This will represent them as a learner. They need to leave room either side for a column of writing.

They should then put a heading at the top of each side; strengths on one side and weaknesses on the other. Ask them to consider themselves as a learner and then jot down selected learning areas under each heading. As they address a learning need over time it can be written across the body and then be ticked off. This gives a clear picture of their learning journey.

Diagram 2 – My interests, activities and hobbies

Ask mentees to make a list or a spider diagram of all their other extra-curricular activities and pastimes. These should include team activities, group membership, leadership roles, positions of responsibility, Duke of Edinburgh award, music, sport, dance, voluntary work, hobbies, current affairs awareness, general knowledge and languages spoken. This will then allow them to consider if they are too busy or if they wish to build on any of their activities, maybe even as a future career. Some mentees may have almost nothing on their list, which provides a good opportunity for them to consider what they could do.

Diagram 3 – My passions and enthusiasms

Mentees can choose how they wish to depict this area. Most prefer to use a mind map. Ask them to jot down over the page, in a series of bubbles, the areas or subjects that enthuse them the most, those which they may pursue in the future. Some will have just one or two, others will have several. Then, considering each area individually, to surround each bubble with a series of lines itemising the evidence of what they are doing to take their passion forwards. If they are not doing anything then they should think what they could do and write this down, using a different colour. They can then choose one idea to pursue as a target.

DIAGRAM 1 – Me as a learner

Strengths

- Perfectionist

- Determination to succeed

- Logical thinking

- Realistic open-minded

- Creative

Weaknesses

- Meeting Deadlines

- Ability to accept negative feedback

- Never wanting to fail

- Rendering work too complicated

- Trying to simultaneously manage too many projects

DIAGRAM 2 - My interests, activities and hobbies

Playing drums, grade 8

Playing Piano, grade 4

Singing in a choir or quartet

Play in orchestra and wind band

Trying different logical puzzles such as the Rubik's cube

Engaging with other people

Analysing everyday products and creating a theoretical re-design

Active Christian and follower of Jesus

Going to church multiple times a week

Looking at new technology and the market influence

Driving along country roads

Taking landscape and light photography

DIAGRAM 3 – My passions and enthusiasms

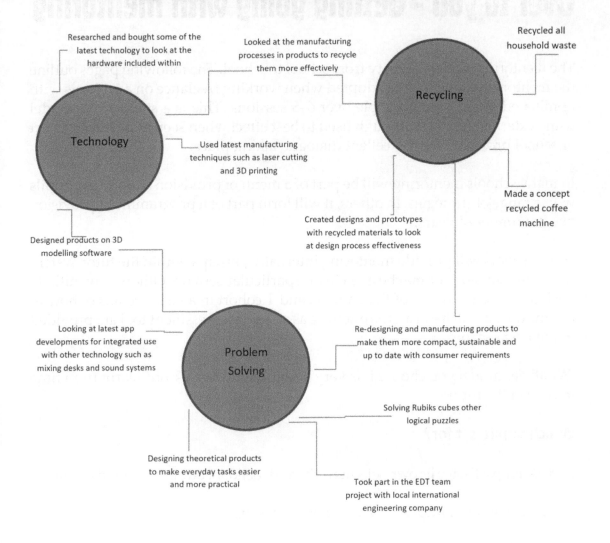

Researched and bought some of the latest technology to look at the hardware included within

Looked at the manufacturing processes in products to recycle them more effectively

Recycled all household waste

Technology

Recycling

Used latest manufacturing techniques such as laser cutting and 3D printing

Made a concept recycled coffee machine

Designed products on 3D modelling software

Created designs and prototypes with recycled materials to look at design process effectiveness

Looking at latest app developments for integrated use with other technology such as mixing desks and sound systems

Problem Solving

Re-designing and manufacturing products to make them more compact, sustainable and up to date with consumer requirements

Solving Rubiks cubes other logical puzzles

Designing theoretical products to make everyday tasks easier and more practical

Took part in the EDT team project with local international engineering company

Over to you - Getting going with mentoring

The mentoring model will vary from school to school. The following pages outline the mentoring model I have adopted when working freelance on a 1:1 basis with nominated gifted young people over 6–8 sessions. This is a stand-alone model using external mentors although used to best effect when seen as an integral part of school provision with excellent dialogue taking place.

In many schools mentoring will be part of a menu of provision supporting pupils with a range of strategies. In others, it will form part of a programme of provision over a number of years.

Some schools will provide mentoring internally perhaps within the tutor system over a few sessions or maybe even in one particular session. Others may initially wish to assess the needs of the entire G and T cohort in a year. Details of how to use the questionnaire in a group setting as an initial assessment tool are provided in the next section.

Whatever model you choose it is very helpful to revisit lessons learnt from time to time in the future.

Which pupils is it for?

Each setting will have its own selection criteria dependant on aim, time and resources.

Schools may select pupils for a number of reasons:

- High potential but low motivation in one or more areas
- Under-achievement
- To monitor the provision for and well-being of a particular cohort of gifted pupils
- To investigate, compare and understand the performance of gifted pupils in different groupings
- To investigate the needs of the quiet pupil
- To ensure the needs of the disadvantaged gifted pupil are being met

Pupils may self-select to improve self-awareness and personal performance. They value the listening ear, the accountability and the support in overcoming barriers.

Parents could nominate their child, with their agreement.

NB Some pupils will be better served by other services i.e. counselling or other specialist support. A mentee needs to be willing and able to reflect, discuss and be part of the solution.

Who is a suitable mentor?

A mentor needs to be someone the mentee trusts and with whom they will openly share their learning journey. This could be a member of the school staff. However, my experience has shown that they are much more honest and at ease with a non-school employee. The mentee needs to be able to reflect on their own performance and to feel safe in voicing concerns and addressing any barriers including those caused by school systems and staff.

The mentor could be a governor, volunteer or paid professional. The key factor is that the mentor is fully trained in the needs and possible issues facing the gifted pupil. Every session will provide new learning opportunities. They must be positive, non-judgemental, open-minded when problem-solving, kind and empathetic; a champion of the needs of gifted pupils. A CRB check is essential.

Initially it could be useful to allow a governor/volunteer to trial this support on a small scale, to measure possible impact. However, as there are many possible facets to the needs of a gifted pupil and many sessions are necessary to gain a detailed and useful awareness, a trained and paid mentor is strongly advised.

A possible cost-effective solution would be to share a trained mentor between several schools as demand for this service will vary across time.

There should always be a named staff member, the link teacher, with overall responsibility for the mentoring scheme. This will be an essential support network for the mentor and demonstrate to the mentee that the school values this type of support.

Overall Method

Mentoring is on a 1:1 basis.

It is essential that the meeting takes place in a quiet, private space where the mentee feels able to share their thoughts and concerns.

Each session lasts about 25–30 minutes.

6–8 sessions are generally sufficient to build trust, reflect and address specific issues. This could be extended in individual cases, some pupils take a while to open up and some issues take longer to address.

Each session ideally takes place fortnightly but weekly is also possible. If several mentees are being seen one after the other then consideration should be given, on consultation with the school and mentee, to changing the order of their appointments from week to week so that the same lesson, or part of it, is not missed each time. This should be clearly noted in the pupil's planner. Some mentees benefit from strategies on how to remember appointments.

In all schools there needs to be a clear policy on confidentiality. It is essential for the mentee to understand that any Child Protection issues will have to be referred. Beyond this all pupils should feel at ease to share any barriers to learning.

Mentoring will stem from the Questionnaire (see 'The Questionnaire – my valuable assessment tool').

The pupil needs to be assured that their comments will not be referred onwards without their permission. This enables the pupil to share openly and the targets then formulated are ones with which they feel comfortable and which are most likely to impact positively on barriers discussed in confidence. They may however allow or even ask the mentor to pass on certain comments after they have together agreed suitable wording. It is very important that the mentee feels they can trust the mentor.

It is important that mentees know they can ask to terminate these sessions if they wish and that the mentor can also do so should the mentee not engage with the process. On occasion it may also be useful to finish a session early if the mentee is struggling to make good use of the session.

Session by session

1. At the initial meeting mentor and mentee briefly introduce themselves. They then work through the questionnaire together. The mentor should ask the initial questions and any others which do not have a numerical rating. Clear instructions for each statement are described across this book.The mentee may also wish to seek clarification or to reflect a little when scoring the other statements. There may be time for initial reflection on the scoring so far. As a first target, the mentee should be asked to complete the first diagram from 3 useful diagrams before the next session.

2. Prior to the next session the mentor should read through the questionnaire making a personal note of any areas for discussion. They should also be provided with relevant data from the school i.e. last school report showing motivation levels, predicted grades and current grades.

3. At the next and subsequent sessions mentor and mentee unpick the answers in more detail. As they go along, the mentor should highlight each area which could benefit from further discussion. Using the highlighted questionnaire, the learner diagram and the potential discussion focus listed at the end of the questionnaire, mentee and mentor should decide together which area to address first. Consideration of the school report with the mentee may also be useful. Discussions should generally be pupil-lead. There should be an emphasis on encouragement and support.

4. The mentor should make notes at each session to aid clarity and to enable on-going reflection. Mentees value greatly the fact that someone writes down what they say.

   By the end of each session the mentee, with the help of the mentor, should come up with a SMART target to meet an agreed objective. This should be achievable by the next session. It will generally involve a learning skill in just one subject area. The target should be written in the planner so that mentee, parent and tutor are aware of the agreed target.

   Sometimes the mentee may have identified that there is a personal issue with a certain lesson or teacher style. Some mentees feel brave enough to talk this through face-to-face straightaway. However, often they are happy for the mentor to offer to make contact with this teacher as a means of modelling positive communication. (Generally the mentee can be encouraged to do this

135

independently when the occasion next arises.) It is important that the school has set up an agreed method of communication for the mentor, e.g. email. There may also be more general issues mentioned and with the permission of the mentee the mentor can then mention these to the member of staff overseeing the mentoring.

Mentees should be asked to complete the other two useful diagrams at some point during the mentoring period as an additional aid to discussion. The contents of these may also provide material for the formulation of targets.

5. Sometimes mentees will, initially at least, forget to address the target by the next session. The mentor should draw their attention to the fact that the sessions are for their benefit and not that of the mentor. Usually this will lead to renewed determination to progress. Occasionally a mentee will consistently not address the target at all. It is then important to review the purpose of the sessions and the targets and to discuss whether the sessions should continue. The mentor should also contact the school to advise them of the situation. The school may be able to suggest helpful strategies or perhaps this will highlight the need for alternative support.

6. During the sessions it may become clear that several mentees have the same issues. The mentor should discuss with the mentees and the school the possibility of addressing this one issue in a group setting. This would allow a wider range of solutions to be suggested and would also address possible feelings of isolation.

7. At the end of the sessions the mentor should ask the mentee to evaluate the sessions; Were sessions useful? What has been the most helpful? Could they have been improved in any way? How will they personally take their learning forward?

The mentor should ensure the mentee understands the full use of the three useful diagrams and ask them to continue to use them to aid their reflection and learning goals.

Links with staff

All adults who teach the mentee should be aware they are attending mentoring sessions. They can give welcome encouragement. The tutor alone will be aware of all the targets written in the planner. Other teachers will be aware of a target that relates to their lessons. It would be helpful if these staff support the mentee if they wish to discuss learning in their subject and/or wish to make suggestions i.e. to move places, to negotiate a revised date for submission of work when the homework schedule is overloaded, to allow more pupil involvement in lessons. The mentor will have discussed with the pupil when and how to address any issues to maximise success.

It would be very helpful to the mentor to receive from staff any comments, suggestions, anecdotal evidence or data which could assist or demonstrate progress. This not only assists the mentee but provides positive reinforcement for the mentor – it can otherwise be a lonely role. The mentor should be treated as part of the team.

Links with parents

In all schools parental permission should be sought before mentoring takes place. It is also helpful to provide information on how this will work and the rationale. This could be in writing or, where a number of pupils are to be mentored, in a specific parents' meeting if this is deemed appropriate.

In a secondary setting mentoring is often school based and the questionnaire is completed by the pupil alone. However, greater parental involvement could prove highly beneficial. This should be in consultation with the mentee. Parental support in the completion of targets would be of great value. Consideration could be given to a final report highlighting targets and successes. Care must be taken not to compromise pupil confidentiality.

The formation of a support group for the parents of gifted children is very helpful. This will allow sharing of experiences, resources, ideas and address isolation. Input by the school on school systems, a pupil perspective and input from a Mentor on possible issues and thoughts on how parents can support effectively are also very useful. This could be offered by year group as different challenges are faced from year to year or, to maximise turn out, perhaps by key stage. The group should meet at least annually. Parents should be consulted on possible items to be included.

Integral part of the school system

It is essential that the mentoring service is seen by all as a vital part of school provision and not as an add-on.

Management of the service should be by a member of the SLT with reference to the G and T co-ordinator. All staff should be aware of the existence and benefits of the service and be involved in nomination of potential mentees and assessment of the progress of those mentees with whom they have contact. This should include both teaching and non-teaching staff.

It is important that a simple system is in place to enable the mentor to receive relevant feedback both in data and anecdotal form. This will significantly increase impact.

Overall findings should form part of on-going staff INSET so that issues can be addressed and system changes made where necessary. Over time this may lessen the need for individual mentoring sessions.

The number of youngsters needing mentoring may fluctuate greatly across time. Thought should be given to sharing the expertise and cost of the mentor across schools.

A clear system should be in place to advise the mentor of relevant systems and policies i.e. behaviour, learning and teaching, G and T, SEN, child protection, also of TD days, closure days, school trips and pupil absence. There should also be a clear policy on alerting the school when mentees do not attend sessions and, as some at times forget, a way of quickly finding them.

Questionnaire as a group assessment tool

The questionnaire is primarily designed to be used on an individual basis. However, it can successfully be used in a group setting to allow schools to obtain a quick overview of need across a particular G and T cohort in the school or across the entire school G and T population. Answers obtained will not be as precise as those from 1:1 sessions as there may be a variation in pupil interpretation of the questions. However, once the data is tabled, it will give a clear picture of trends by gender and year group and across the school and will highlight those pupils who have the greatest need.

This assessment method requires 45–60 minutes, one lesson. Groups of no more than 24 should be asked to sit with a partner with whom they are happy to talk. If there is an uneven number of pupils then one group of three is preferable to the facilitator taking part as they are likely to be asked for clarification by some pupils during questionnaire completion.

The facilitator should ask the pairs of pupils to swap scripts and explain that for the initial section one will play the mentor and the other the mentee and then they will swap roles. The rationale behind this is that in conversation, when the questioner is asking for clarification and precision, deeper reflection will take place and it will be easier for the respondent to find a meaningful answer to all questions. The facilitator should run through the questions in the first section, with reference to the notes in each section of this book, so that pupils are clear what is being asked. The pupils should then complete this section. It will take about ten minutes for the pairs to ask the questions and complete the answers for their partner.

About your learning

The pupils should each now have their own script and score the statements in the section on resilience, stopping at the final question – What would you like to learn about? It is useful to point out that some questions are worded 'back to front' to stop pupils whizzing through them without due thought. It should be emphasised that you are looking for considered responses. There will still be some pupils who complete this extremely quickly. They would benefit from starting to unpick their scoring with their partner.

At the end of the section, when all pupils are ready, you should talk through the question using the explanation given earlier in the book. Pupils can then talk through their answers with their partner before writing their response. A few minutes should then be spent allowing for feedback. The rest of the questionnaire should be completed in the same way. When completing the question on 'How could we make school/learning even better?' it is best not to offer possible suggestions as they will undoubtedly skew the responses.

Other factors

It is important to stress that this section is more personal and pupils are free not to answer. In my experience, they always complete it, some in great depth. They relish the opportunity to share their life. It is crucial to read the answers in this section straight after the session to check for any 'child protection' issues or more likely issues which immediately need a listening ear.

What would you like to gain from the mentoring sessions?

In place of the final question, schools seeking an overview and not necessarily considering a full mentoring scheme could ask, thinking about all your responses, what one thing would help you most with your learning?

In any remaining time it is extremely useful to ask pupils for their overall thoughts about the statements. Was there anything which surprised them? Did any particular statement jump out at them? Did they recognise themselves in a particular statement? Pupils who had time to unpick their scoring may also be able to provide some useful insights. For many it will be the first time they have truly reflected on their learning and their needs as a gifted pupil. As one pupil told me 'I had never thought about my learning in this way and I can now see how helpful it is.'

Notes

Notes

Notes

Notes

Notes

Notes